FROM
SHATTERED
TO WHOLE

FROM
SHATTERED
TO WHOLE

Andrea Foxcroft

This book shares the author's own recollections and memories. She has done her best to be faithful to her experiences, but memory is imperfect. She has also done her best to present her journey and the other people in it in the most honest, positive light.

Printed in the United States of America
Published in Hellertown, PA
Cover design by Anna Magruder
Cover art by Ella Stover
Library of Congress Control Number 2025911886
ISBN 979-8-89420-056-9
For more information or to place bulk orders, contact the author or the publisher at Jennifer@BrightCommunications.net.

Bright
COMMUNICATIONS

To My Savior, My Creator, My God, My Everything,
who is worthy of all glory, honor, and praise

Part One: The Beginning

Chapter 1

I met Matt in the spring of 2011 in Perryville, Maryland, where we both worked in sales for local newspapers. The salespeople were a friendly bunch, and we often had work dinners and hung out after hours.

From the very first moment I met Matt, I knew he was unique. His personality screamed "confidence!" He was funny and charismatic, and yes, a little arrogant. But that made him unusual to me. He also made me laugh so much.

I could tell that Matt had a huge crush on me because from day one, he began flirting with me. He asked me out for *months*. He refused to accept my answer—which was always no. He was crazy persistent and kept asking. I don't think anyone had ever told him no before.

It wasn't that I didn't *like* Matt. It wasn't even that I wasn't attracted to him. But I'm ten years older than he is. Plus, I was a young mom with three daughters from my first marriage. At the time, my first daughter, Kayla, was fifteen years old; my second daughter, Alyssa, was twelve years old; and my baby girl, Arabella, was just five years old.

Although I was aware of the age gap between Matt and me, age is just a number. I didn't feel a *maturity* gap. People who watch us on YouTube might think Matt is youthful and silly, but he's actually an old soul. Back when we first met, he seemed a lot older than his biological age. That was probably the reason we were attracted to each other. We were the same "real age."

As the months wore on, the chasing game continued as Matt pursued me.

"Will you go out with me?"

"No."

"Now will you go out with me?"

"No."

Finally, I ran out of willpower. I gave in and said yes. After all of that asking, Matt had convinced me that he was invested and loyal. And he was certainly persistent.

For our first date, we went to Sands Casino—along with some coworkers. When we got there, Matt and I took off on our own. I did not know how to play craps, so Matt taught me. I had beginner's luck. I rolled the dice for almost an hour, and I made a lot of money for all the players. Matt was betting on me too, and we walked away with a few thousand dollars each. That was a thrilling experience.

I had never felt so alive as when I was with Matt. We talked a lot when we worked, and I felt like I was getting to know him better and better.

But our second date blew my mind. We had planned to go out, but I had no idea what we were going to be doing. We were in Salisbury, Maryland, for work, but we were off that day.

"Go change into your bathing suit," Matt said.

"Why?" I asked.

"It's a surprise!" Matt said.

When we got into the car and Matt started driving, I noticed we were headed toward Ocean City, Maryland, which isn't far from Salisbury. Matt pulled into a parking lot with a sign that said, "Jet skiing and parasailing." I was horrified because I was wearing a bikini.

"What are we doing here?" I asked, already knowing the answer.

"We're going jet skiing and parasailing," Matt said cheerfully.

"Whoa," I said.

We rented a jet ski, and I drove us first, just around the bay. I was doing a great job driving, and my confidence grew.

Then we switched. Matt is fearless, and his crazy turns had me holding on to him for dear life. I was terrified I was going to fall off. I gripped the handles so hard that my arms still hurt the next day. Matt playfully tried to throw me off a few times. I was furious, but at the same time, I was laughing and having the time of my life.

When Matt and I were done jet skiing, we headed over to the boat for parasailing. We got into harnesses, sailed out to the sea, then they pushed us off the boat. Matt and I soared higher and higher into the air. It was so peaceful and calm up there. We were smiling and holding hands. It was surreal. Blissful. In that quiet, beautiful moment, I realized that I had caught feelings for Matt. I hadn't planned that, but I felt like I was no longer in control of my feelings, which was unnerving. I was falling in love with Matt.

The almost-a-year of dating Matt was the most fun I had ever had with anyone in my life. I can't say I've dated a lot. I married my high school sweetheart, and I really never went out with anyone else. At thirty-two years old, I had never experienced what I was experiencing with Matt.

As Matt and I got to know each other, we discovered that we enjoyed a lot of the same things. We both loved sports, traveling, amusement parks, singing karaoke, going to the movies and the beach. Most of all, we loved being together.

Initially, Matt and I saw each other two or three times a week. But that soon became four to six days a week.

Have you ever had the time of your life? I was, and I had never experienced that before. Everything about my relationship with Matt was exciting and new. Every experience, every moment was special. To this day, I cherish every memory of that time.

Matt and I were living each day bursting with love and anticipation. I felt so blessed to have found the love of my life. After that, we were inseparable. It felt like if we didn't see each other, we couldn't breathe. We had that rare relationship where we were lovers and also best friends. We would watch football and baseball together. We would laugh and do crazy, spontaneous things. We would wake up on a beautiful day and decide to drive hours away to Gettysburg, Pennsylvania, or Williamsburg, Virginia, just to have fun and be together.

But as Matt and I grew closer, I think he was nervous to meet my daughters. They met one day at my best friend's house. Although my daughters thought it was weird at first that I'm older than Matt, he made them laugh, and they loved his humor right away. My three daughters all have silly, witty senses of humor, and from the start, Matt was so much fun with them. We all went to amusement parks, baseball games, and the movies.

Matt loved my daughters right away too. Early on, when Matt learned how much my youngest daughter, Bella, loves LEGO sets, he started taking her to the LEGO store often to buy more sets. Looking back, I think Matt was fascinated by Bella's ability to put together LEGO sets and puzzles so quickly. As far as puzzles go, the more pieces they contained the better for Bella.

After Matt and I dated for a year, we rented a house in Pasadena, Maryland, and moved in together. Even though Matt and my daughters liked each other, moving in together required a little adjustment by everyone. It took some time to begin to function as a family. My daughters were used to being parented solely by me. They only saw their dad every few months.

At first, Matt tried to stay out of the disciplinary actions because he didn't want to step on anyone's toes. That wasn't difficult with my youngest daughter, but it was more difficult with my older daughters. They gave me a hard time. Teenagers can be very "fun" to parent. So Matt hung back, acting like an uncle to my older daughters, while he was more of a stepdad to my youngest, Bella. He took her to baseball games, helped her with homework, and put together puzzles and LEGO sets with her.

Eventually, as my other daughters got older, they started to see Matt as their stepdad too. We all loved playing board games together. We'd have to keep an eye on Matt because he'd cheat sometimes. We also enjoyed going to the movies, having dinner at Matt's parents' house, and just hanging out. Our modern family just *worked*.

I was extremely grateful that Matt loved my daughters, and in time, my daughters grew to love Matt too. I can imagine that it's difficult to be in a relationship with someone who has children who are not your biological children. Matt was so supportive of my daughters in every way. I remember thinking all the time, *I don't know how I got so lucky.*

After being together for seven years, Matt and I were married on December 26, 2017, in West Palm Beach, Florida. It was an intimate gathering of family.

Our wedding was a dream come true. After our first year together, I had a dream that I married Matt on a beach. When I told Matt's mom about my dream, she told me she wanted to create that. I'm so lucky to have such an amazing mother-in-law. She has been so supportive of me and my daughters from the beginning. I gave her free rein over the planning. She picked out my dress and my daughters' dresses—all very bohemian. She planned our reception in Lake Worth at a high-end

Italian restaurant. She even picked our wedding song: Ed Sheeran's "Perfect."

My mother-in-law kept that a secret though, and when I heard the first notes, I almost cried with joy. Matt and I danced, and it really was perfect. We were both so happy. It was a very special day.

Chapter 2

Matt's newspaper sales job required him to work odd hours and also to travel a lot. So in 2015, he decided he would find another job where he would not have to travel. Matt started working for a small, local RV dealer. He needed a job that would allow him to leave by a certain time to make room for his side gig: beer vending. He worked part-time as a beer vendor for the Washington Nationals baseball team and the Capitals hockey team. Luckily, the drive from the RV dealership to Washington DC was only 45 minutes.

Matt loved beer vending, which he had started in 2013 as a seasonal job. He only worked during baseball and hockey seasons. He was one of the top sellers. Matt could sell ice to Eskimos. He did part-time beer vending up to 2019.

Matt was drawn to work in the RV industry because he honestly thought RVs were really cool. And he knew selling RVs would be better than selling cars—or at least more interesting. Back then, I never imagined he would love RVs so much.

At that time, I also sold RVs part time, and I worked with Matt at many RV shows.

After Matt and I sold RVs for a few months, he said, "I want to make videos about RVs. They could help with RV sales. Maybe I could start a YouTube channel."

At the time, I thought it was a good idea—or at least a worthwhile experiment. I knew that it was something

Matt wanted to do. He always has really good ideas. Sometimes they have been a little crazy, but I always supported him.

Matt started by filming detailed RV reviews on a channel called Leo's Vacation Center, which was started by the RV dealer we worked for. Matt enjoyed creating and filming the videos, but he quickly ran out of RVs to review at the small dealership. He didn't quite like the format or the growth of the channel, but he kept at it for a few years.

I think what kept Matt at it was that he *did* like being on camera and educating RV consumers. He became a full-on RV nerd. He got so familiar with RVs that he could easily identify RV makes and models just by seeing the front of one. Matt got so knowledgeable that he began to dream about starting his *own* YouTube channel—where he could design the format and propel the growth.

Back then, Matt was a huge fan of an extremely successful entrepreneur and motivational speaker named Gary V. In 2018, Matt attended one of Gary V's events about networking and growing your business. At that event, Matt had the epiphany for what would become one of the most popular features of his channel: The three things he likes and the three things he dislikes about an RV.

Part of Matt's participation in Gary V's event was a one-on-one consultation with Gary. That's where the name "Matt's RV Reviews" was born.

When Matt got home and told me about it, I thought, *That sounds great.* "You could definitely do it," I said.

"It's going to be a huge channel," Matt said confidently.

I remember smiling to myself because I believed in him, and I believed he was right. I was really proud of him. And I wanted all his dreams to come true.

Chapter 3

Previously, Matt's YouTube video creation had been a one-man show. He had researched, starred in, and even filmed his own videos. But he was ready to expand, so he began looking for someone *else* to film him reviewing the RVs.

Matt didn't have to look far for a cameraperson. He hired his receptionist and assistant at Leo's Vacation Center, a talented young woman named Jen.

That was the start of our video story! Matt threw all his passion, energy, and time into those videos. He did all the planning, starring, editing, publishing, and social media. It was a good thing Matt is very energetic and ambitious because it was *a lot* of work. And Matt did all that, *plus* his RV sales job *and* his beer vending side gig.

At the time, I tried to support Matt in any way he needed me. He would run ideas by me and ask for my opinions. I was still raising my three daughters, which kept me busy. But I would take care of some of Matt's RV customers to help him out so he still got the sales. I worked the weekends at Leo's. Matt is so good at selling that he had lots of customers. At home, I handled everything—the housework, yardwork, laundry, and cooking—because I wanted to make things easier for Matt.

Matt's goals were to grow the channel and to make it special. But he still had that one huge problem: very little inventory. We knew the channel couldn't grow without a bigger inventory to review, which meant we needed to be at a much larger dealership. We knew we would have to move if we wanted the channel to grow.

For Christmas 2017, Matt and I drove to Florida to celebrate the holidays with his mom. We borrowed a motor home from our work, which was one of the best perks of selling RVs. Like all our RV trips, it was fantastic.

The memories you make RVing are priceless and unforgettable. Our family had the most fun on our RV trips. Over the years, we've taken at least eight trips as a family. I'm grateful my daughters experienced those family vacations. I know they look back on them fondly. Hopefully one day when my daughters have children of their own, they will remember those good times and be inspired to plan similar experiences with their own families.

Matt and I always enjoyed ourselves on RV trips. I would sit in the co-captain's chair and be his backseat driver. We would laugh and sing all the way to Florida. We began to look forward to those road trips. Along the way, we would often camp at small, local campgrounds because we all loved the friendly RV community so much.

Besides the five of us, our daughters would often bring friends on our RV trips. We'd have between three and six girls on our trips, plus me and Matt!

Another perk of RVing is taking your pets. Back then, our tabby cat, Ezra, was one year old, and our rescue calico, Mochi, was about three years old. They often came along. We kept the litterbox in the master bedroom while in transit. Then, when the slides were open, we kept it in the shower because we didn't use the shower. We showered in the campground bath houses.

Those were great times, and I miss those days. If you ever have the opportunity to rent or buy an RV, do it! It's worth it. You can do so much traveling—in comfort.

Back in 2018, after another wonderful Christmas visit with Matt's mom, we were heading home to Maryland. Matt wanted to stop in Richmond, Virginia, to check out an RV dealership called General RV. It was the closest General RV dealership to us, around three hours from our home. Matt wanted to see what the dealership looked like and to learn how they ran things.

Matt spent some time in the dealership, walking around and talking with the salespeople. He seemed to like General RV. It was a very large dealership with plenty of inventory. General RV also had a stellar reputation, which was important to Matt.

In the New Year, 2019, things started to accelerate. Matt traveled to General RV's headquarters in Florida for a job interview. He mentioned that he was making YouTube RV videos and that if he were hired by General RV, he would still want to record them.

That was not an issue for General RV. In fact, they were fully on board—as long as Matt did his sales job first. Matt was hired to do RV sales for the General RV's Ocala, Florida, dealership.

Of course, that meant we were moving to Florida! We were all excited—except Bella, who was a preteen at the time and did not want to leave her friends. To this day, Bella runs back to Maryland whenever she can because all of her BFFs still live there.

While Matt was in Florida for his interview, he also met with a Realtor. The very first house he looked at in Oxford, Florida, was perfect for our family. Matt Facetimed me so I could see the house. I loved it right away. On the spot, we decided that was *the* house. It felt like fate was smiling on us.

We moved to Florida in the late summer of 2019. We packed up and left Maryland—never looking back. Jen and her husband, Wil, helped us move down to Florida.

After the big move, Matt said to Jen and Wil, "Wouldn't it be amazing if our channel got big?"

All four of us started cracking up.

"Yeah, right," Matt said. "We could hire you both full-time one day."

Little did we know: We were manifesting our future.

Chapter 4

After our family settled into our new home in Florida and got everyone situated, life started to get back to normal. Matt began his new job as a salesman at General RV in Ocala.

One day, Matt said, "I need you to record me."

"Of course I will," I said.

Filming Matt was a little chaotic at first. It can be challenging working with your spouse! Also it took me a little bit to learn how to use the GoPro. In the beginning, I had no idea what I was doing. And there was no one around to teach me! So I had to learn by trial and error. But the more I used the camera, the more comfortable I became. I always watched the videos afterward to see what I could improve upon. Also, I asked for and listened to constructive criticism. It was a steep learning curve, but I got the hang of it.

Pretty soon, Matt and I started to record a couple of videos a few days a week. Back then, Matt's RV Reviews had around 7,000 YouTube subscribers. In the beginning videos (pre-COVID-19 pandemic), I didn't want to be on camera, so Matt would talk to me and ask for my opinion on the RVs while I remained comfortably behind the camera.

But after a few weeks, without warning, Matt grabbed the camera from me and turned it on me! "Andrea, say hi to everyone!" he exclaimed cheerfully. Then he said, "Everyone, say hi to Andrea!"

"Hi," I said, shocked and surprised. That was the start of me being on camera too. After that, little by little, I would interact in the videos as Matt included me more and more.

Back then, Matt and I were a videoing team of two—just us. We did all the planning, preparations, filming, and editing. Truth be told, we were having fun doing them ourselves. We began to get really good feedback from our YouTube subscribers, who often said that they liked our chemistry together and seeing a married couple doing reviews, each sharing their own opinions. I began reviewing parts of the RVs, such as the kitchen, and I'd also give my opinions at the end of each video, helping Matt share our three likes and our three dislikes.

Matt and I were having a blast doing RV reviews. Matt is hilarious most of the time—both on and off camera. He has no filter. He is a brutally honest, straight shooter.

At that time, the growth of Matt's RV Reviews was good. Matt was trying to figure out the YouTube algorithm. We began to experiment with the channel, trying to puzzle out things like: How often should we upload videos? What's the best day of the week and time of the day to upload? After months of experimentation, Matt figured out the process that was best for us. We posted a new video every other day. That seemed to be the magic pacing, and our channel grew more quickly after that.

Then the COVID-19 pandemic hit. With so much uncertainty and panic, most RV dealerships shut down. The whole RV industry eventually closed for a little while, except for the General RV dealerships in Florida, which remained open.

Matt sold 10 RVs in February 2020, largely due to our YouTube channel and mostly from out-of-state subscribers. By then we had around 20,000 YouTube subscribers. We were grateful that our channel sustained us through the pandemic.

Then the RV boom hit! People were getting into RVs for travel because it seemed safer than other options. Airplanes and other public transportation had very strict protocols, as did most hotels, so the RV industry went crazy! It seemed like all the RV inventory in Florida was selling out. People from all over were buying RVs. Our YouTube channel gained more and more subscribers, and soon we were at 55,000 subs. That is rapid growth for any channel.

Matt was doing an amazing job with RV sales. He got very busy with all the leads from our channel. In fact, it was too much for him to handle, so he began transferring leads to other trusted salespeople. By the end of 2020, we were almost at 100,000 subscribers.

Because our channel was thriving, Matt and I got to travel all over the country to record RV reviews. We had so much fun visiting different General RV dealership locations in other states. We hit the 100k subscribers milestone in January 2021. It was amazing to receive our silver YouTube Play Button plaque. I can still see Matt's face when he opened up that box like it was yesterday. He was so excited and happy. It was a very memorable time for us, especially because we had accomplished it together. We were grateful to have come so far in such a short time.

But we did not get there on our own. We love our subscribers. They are so loyal and supportive, and despite all the changes our channel has gone through over the years, they have always been patient. Our channel's success is all because of them. Our audience is special, and we love interacting with them.

Chapter 5

After a year and a half with General RV, Matt and I decided to change dealerships again. We needed to see how another big dealer would handle our leads. We wondered if they could keep up with the internet leads coming through and turning them into sales. Back then, General RV was unfamiliar with the YouTube influencer way of marketing. I think they were surprised at how well we did the first year.

But after that, they couldn't agree to increasing our terms, so we decided to leave General RV. No hard feelings. We loved General RV. I just don't think they were ready for influencer marketing yet. We shook hands with no burnt bridges or bad feelings.

Although General RV had a large presence on the east coast and central United States, Matt and I went to RV One, which is now Blue Compass, which was nationwide. We worked at their Tampa location, right down the street from General RV, for one year to grow more as a team and channel. At that point, our manifestation came true, and we hired Jen and Wil to work for Matt's RV Reviews.

At Blue Compass, Matt's job was strictly to do videos. He wasn't working as an RV salesman; however, we *were* paid bonuses for leads that came from our channel and converted into sales. Moving to a family-owned dealer with that kind of magnitude and a trusted name was exactly what our channel needed.

Because our channel was growing so fast, Matt and I started a second, spin-off channel to review towable RVs, called Matt's RV Reviews Towables. The audience for towable RVs is largely different than the audience for motorized RVs. Unfortunately, filming for that channel became a little too much for me, so we hired Wil to help film.

Thank God for Wil. He loves RVs, and he is very knowledgeable, so that channel was the perfect fit for him. Matt and Will did batch recording of those videos, where they would meet and record enough videos for a few months.

At the time, we promoted Jen to Creative Director. She began editing our videos, and she also designed our website, MattsRVReviews.com. We were so lucky to have such talented friends to help and support us. They kept us straight and organized.

By late winter 2022, Matt's RV Reviews hit 200k subs. After careful consideration, Matt and I decided to go *back* to General RV in 2023. By that time, General had a better, more established internet sales team. They took care of our customers, so most leads translated into sales. Their closing ratio of our leads to sales was really impressive. Matt and I felt that General RV had the best prices too. The vast majority of our customers were very happy with their purchase.

Even though Matt and I had to make some sacrifices to switch back to General RV, it was totally worth it. We knew that the move would benefit our customers and channel, setting us up for future success.

Throughout 2022 and 2023, Matt and I were constantly on the move, traveling all over the country, filming and attending rallies, meet and greets, and of course RV shows. Wherever we were, my very imaginative, creative husband came up with all kinds of ideas. This normally happened when he was in the shower—his best place of inspiration.

One of Matt's ideas was to partner with large sponsors. We signed with RVMattress.com, Lippert Components (a global manufacturer and supplier of RV, marine, and automotive products), and RV Life (an RV trip planner).

Another one of Matt's ideas was to share the sales price of the RV we were reviewing in our videos. RV One didn't allow us to do that, but now General RV did. That set us apart from other RV reviews on YouTube.

It was in the shower where Matt got his biggest idea yet—to develop a new RV black tank cleaner. The RV's black tank is the holding tank where all the toilet waste goes. (The grey tank is the holding tank for your shower and sink water.) In the RV black tank, the waste and toilet paper need to be liquified so that it will come out of the black tank through the sewer hose. Because an RV is a house on wheels, the septic system is portable, which complicates all of these processes!

Matt liked the idea of creating a new black tank cleaner because it aligned with his brand—the Prime Pooping Position. If you've seen Matt's RV Reviews, when we review an RV, Matt sits on the toilet and announces if the toilet is in the Prime Pooping Position—or not (womp, womp, womp).

To develop our black tank cleaner, Matt and I did a lot of research. First, we identified the fifteen top-rated RV black tank treatments, then we bought containers of each. We bought fifteen plastic bins with tops, lined them up in our garage, and numbered them one through fifteen. We put the same amount of water, dog poop, and RV toilet paper into each of them. Then we tested a different product in each bin. We recorded the progress of each cleaner at twenty-four hours and again at forty-eight hours.

You can check out our experiment here on our channel.

Surprisingly, only two out of the fifteen black tank treatments performed well and actually did what they were supposed to do. Of those two, we preferred Century Chemical, which is located in Indiana. It's enzyme-based and made in the United States.

Matt negotiated with Century Chemical to create a unique product for us with its own color and smell. They now produce and bottle our product, then ship it to our warehouse, which is also in Indiana.

Matt also found the exact type of bottle we wanted. It has a spout to premeasure the product on one side and a spout on the other side for pouring. Our Creative Director, Jen, designed the label and website for the tank cleaner.

Matt decided to call the product Liquified because it *liquifies* all the waste in the RV's black tank. We started selling Liquified exclusively on Amazon.com because of the ease of working with them and their excellent distribution. Amazon offered the fastest way to begin selling in bulk. Amazon reviews were important to us too. Because we were new to this, it helped that they packaged and shipped our products to the customers. We soon began sending pallets of Liquified to Amazon fulfillment centers all over the United States.

Now life really started to get busy! And Liquified became my husband's baby.

Part Two: The Decision

Chapter 6

Looking back, the decision to start Liquified was the watershed moment in our marriage. Often in life, we don't even realize when we are at a crossroads and that choosing one path instead of the other will set in motion a chain of events you never saw coming.

Matt and I didn't take out any loans to start Liquified. But we did use all the funds we had. That wasn't as stressful as you might think because I knew it was just Matt's way. He is quick-thinking and quick-acting, and he didn't want to wait to apply for loans.

Our marketing plan for Liquified was to capitalize on our successful YouTube channel. We began mentioning Liquified in our videos, often putting bottles of Liquified in the bathroom cabinets to show when we opened the cabinets in our videos. (Surprise! It's Liquified!)

Also, we gifted bottles of Liquified to other YouTube influencers, such as Endless RVing, Five to Go, and Less Junk More Journey. We asked them to try out our product and if they liked it, to make their own videos about how Liquified performed.

From December 2022 to December 2023—Liquified's first year—our company did very well, selling 38,000 bottles on Amazon. With our channel and product growing, Matt and I were always super busy. In September 2022 and then again in 2023, we even went to Germany for Düsseldorf World's Biggest RV Show. Back then, the European RV Market was more innovative than ours.

Matt and I took two of my daughters with us and made the trips working vacations. In 2022, after the show in Germany, we went to France and England. They are such beautiful countries, and I was fascinated by the culture and architecture. I'm definitely a geek for anything historical, and Windsor Castle, the Tower of London, and Stonehenge were my favorite places. I was so happy that we could experience Europe as a family. Traveling to film has always been my favorite thing about my job. It's invigorating and thrilling to see different places.

Wil and Jen met us in Paris. We had the best time and made some amazing memories.

In late fall 2022, we got back from Europe and went right back into the grind. However, Matt and I welcomed all the opportunities and business we were getting. We did our best to juggle everything.

Matt handled most of the Liquified affairs. He had big plans for our little business. The phrase "I can't do it" is not part of his vocabulary.

But on the flip side, Matt and I were struggling to make time for ourselves, and our marriage was starting to suffer. I thought that was normal with starting up a business. We were too busy and tired for each other.

But as time went on, in the winter of 2022, I noticed Matt and I were getting even more distant. We tried to make our monthly date nights. For a few months, we stretched them out to a few-days' getaway. That worked for a few months. Then it became a struggle to coordinate our schedules. After only about three months, date nights became nonexistent.

I didn't feel like I was a priority to Matt anymore. He was so busy with work, work, work. But I tried to tell myself I was overreacting. How could I be upset by his ambition? That is who Matt is. I knew who he was when I married him. I always supported him in dreaming big. I just never thought the businesses would take my place.

I tried to be a little more patient. I could see changes happening all around us. I knew Matt had a lot going on. He was recording at home with me, traveling to record with Wil, working to get Liquified into dealerships and campgrounds, and negotiating with our sponsors. But Matt loves to work, and he is amazing at everything!

The next year, 2023, was a blur for me. The Liquified launch and our channels' growth brought many new opportunities. Suddenly, I felt Matt was gone more than he was home. And even when he was home, he was working. I started to feel alone—and invisible.

I tried to be understanding because I knew everything Matt was doing. But he had Wil as General Manager, Jen as Creative Director, and a third team member dedicated to working with Amazon. With all that extra help, I hoped Matt would find time for us.

I began talking to Matt about this all the time. "I'm so lonely. I feel like I'm losing both my husband and my best friend," I said often.

"It's going to be okay," Matt would say. Then we would hug it out. Matt liked to try to make me feel better. Some nights we would watch TV together. It became difficult to have a conversation because he was constantly on his laptop or phone. That was pretty much the only time I saw him.

The only quality time Matt and I had together was when we were recording. When Matt wasn't traveling, he would work at the dealership, and I would meet him there to record. That was not a good time for us. We began to argue a lot, and it felt like we were becoming strangers. When Matt asked me to go to dinner, it would be so late in the evening that I would say no because I had already eaten. Our communication was not good.

To make matters worse, I started distancing myself from everyone, even my family and friends. Because I didn't feel comfortable talking about my marital problems, which were becoming all-consuming, I didn't feel that I had anyone to talk to.

My only solace was my cellphone. I began spending hours and hours each day out on my patio, reading or shopping on my phone. I felt so helpless, like I had no control over what was happening in my life. I was in my own bubble of loneliness. I became very depressed—not knowing what to do anymore.

I tried to explain to Matt how I felt, but I didn't feel that he was taking me seriously. I knew he didn't like confrontation, and it seemed to me that when I tried to talk with him to figure things out, he would make excuses to get away.

But I knew our marriage was at stake. I knew that we needed a plan to repair it.

After a few weeks, my isolating depression morphed into anger. Our issues really began to affect me. I was irritated—always in a bad mood. That didn't help my marriage.

Nor did it help when I began nagging my husband. But it was difficult to stay quiet when I could see that Matt was so busy that he was missing things. I began reminding him to do things. I *really* did not want to nag him, and I must have sounded like a broken record.

All of my life, I've been a worrywart. But then, more than ever, I felt the weight of the world on my shoulders. I've always lived a fast-paced life, but intuitively I knew I needed to get out of the fast lane. It felt like everything was falling apart. I was alone with no one to talk to.

The only time Matt and I saw each other was when we were recording. We began taking out our problems on each other. It is very difficult to film when you're upset. But I think overall Matt and I were professional. We filmed the videos with brave faces. He could always put on a happy face. He did his job like nothing was going on.

I knew that was far from the truth.

To make matters worse, Matt's work travel was increasing. He would go away for a week, and we would talk maybe twice while he was gone. It was not our best communication, and in fact, it got worse that year. It got to the point where I would call or text, and Matt wouldn't take my call or reply to my text.

Meanwhile, I was home shopping and reading, and frequently walking our dog—not knowing what Matt was doing or if he was even safe. Because of my depression and loneliness, my shopping ballooned out of control. I loved clothes and shoes, and I soon had a cosmetic and skincare addiction. I did not need all these things I was buying. I was being ridiculous! Looking back, I can't believe I let myself go like that. I spent thousands of dollars on makeup and skincare. I'm embarrassed at how I let shopping consume me. It was only temporarily filling the huge void growing inside me.

Maybe Matt isn't interested in me anymore: That thought was always at the back of my mind. Why else would this be happening? I knew he had *some* free time because he would play pickleball or go to the dog park. I didn't understand why Matt wasn't taking me seriously—why he was shutting me out.

But how could I not think that way? Being a woman in the 2020s is extremely hard. We are made to think we must look and act perfectly all the time. Society judges us, and it's even worse when you're on social media.

In 2023, when Matt got home from work trips, I said, "I texted you. Why didn't you text me back?"

"I was so busy," he said. "By the time I got back to the hotel, I was exhausted."

I understood that. Filming all day saps all your energy. I know that Matt and I feel "talked out" sometimes. But what I couldn't understand is why he couldn't at least *text* me. That had never happened before.

This soul-crushing pattern continued for the rest of 2023. Matt and I became more and more estranged. I felt more and more defeated—and less and less hopeful. I was slowly, painfully watching my husband move farther away from me. Even the intimacy between us was strained.

It was excruciating seeing this happen, all the while knowing that I didn't know how to fix it. I just wanted Matt back because I missed him so much. I understood he was busy and going through a lot. Why couldn't he see that I was going through a lot too?

Every time I tried to talk to Matt about this, we would both agree to work on it. And we did. Whenever Matt was home, we went out to dinner a few days a week and spent more time alone. But eventually that stopped again.

I began crying all the time. Matt would be gone for weeks, come home for a week, then leave again. I was so angry and unhappy. The only time I spent with Matt was to record YouTube videos.

In desperation, I began to throw the D word out a lot. I hoped that maybe would get Matt's attention—make him think and prioritize. It wasn't working. In fact, if anything it pushed him away more.

I was determined not to spend the rest of my life alone. But the reality was that's exactly what was happening.

Matt and I were both growing—but not together. We were growing farther and farther apart. Something had shifted in our relationship, and I worried that maybe our marriage was not important to him anymore. Was business his priority now?

I desperately missed the old days when we talked all the time. When we could tell each other anything. When we missed each other if we were apart. When we could not go one day without speaking. When we had fun working together. I missed our family dinners and hanging out with the kids.

Matt and I used to be so close. He was my rock, my best friend, the love of my life. How did everything fall apart so fast?

As 2023 lumbered to a close, my anger morphed into paralysis. I began "shoulding" on myself. I *should* have gone out with Matt more. I *should* have cooked him dinner sometimes. I *should* have learned to play pickleball. I *should* have done more things with him. I *should* have told him how amazing he was and how much I appreciated him. I *should* have been more flexible with his schedule.

Even though some of those things *might* have helped, I began to wonder if Matt could have done things differently too. Did he really need to handle *all* of the business by himself? We had help after all. I worried that maybe he just wanted to work so hard—especially because our marriage was on its last leg. Was he running from the issues because he didn't want to address them?

I sensed Matt and I were hurtling to a breaking point, and we needed to do something. The D word began flying out of my mouth even more.

Today, I wish I never said that word. I regret having said it. Words have incredible power—the power of life or death.

Chapter 7

The beginning of 2024 was very rocky for us. January was a busy month. Every January, we looked forward to the Tampa RV Show. We've attended it for the past four years, and it has always been so fun to be there.

At RV shows, Matt and I have the honor to meet our subscribers and other influencers while our sales team stands behind us, ready to help our customers purchase RVs. It's surreal to meet people who watch our channel. Our subscribers are so sweet and down-to-earth. They naturally, effortlessly became our friends. Even if I only meet subscribers for a few minutes, I feel like I know them. It's an incredible feeling. Matt and I are so fortunate to have such wonderful subscribers.

In early February 2024, shortly after the Tampa RV Show ended, Matt and I took a cruise with our family and friends. I think overall, everyone had a good time. But it felt awkward being with Matt, trying to have conversations and pretending that all was well between us. Perhaps because Matt felt the same awkwardness, he seemed to always be running off without me, doing other things on the cruise. It was like I was not even there. That really hurt—like a punch in the gut. It made me sick to my stomach. I began to feel like I was not his wife, wondering if wishing our marriage could be saved was in vain.

On the cruise, I hoped that Matt and I might have one day to ourselves. He knew how sad and lonely I was, but he didn't sit with me at dinners or on excursions. At one point during the cruise, we got into an argument.

"I want a [D word]," I said. "You have been ignoring me this whole trip. I don't deserve this treatment. If you want to be single, we don't have to continue like this anymore. Is there someone else?" I asked.

"No!" Matt said.

"Maybe it's time to talk about the D word," I replied.

"I don't want that," Matt said quietly. "I'm so sorry. I didn't realize I was leaving you out." Then Matt got down on his knees and said, "I will do everything to save our marriage."

We were both crying and hugging. The love was *absolutely* still there. I felt it.

But still I wondered, *Why is this so difficult? What is going on between us? Obviously, he still loves me.*

I wanted to be optimistic about Matt meeting me halfway and contributing to making it work, but my optimism was sorely misplaced.

After the cruise, Matt and I went home and got back to our lives and work. For a few weeks in March, Matt traveled. I began to really get into my gym, taking Zumba classes five days a week. I vowed to concentrate on getting healthy and losing 30 pounds. I lost 16 pounds in January alone. Zumba was so much fun. I love to dance, and the hour-long classes flew by. The fact that it was high cardio was a bonus.

My Zumba instructors were so supportive of me. Even though they didn't know what was really going on in my life, I think they sensed I was struggling with something. I needed their support so much because our marital problems were getting worse.

April was extremely busy for Matt and me. We had a rally here in Florida for a reality show *RV Unplugged*. But I couldn't attend because my twenty-four-year-old daughter, Alyssa, was diagnosed with multiple sclerosis (MS) at the emergency department and admitted to the hospital for more than a week. I needed to be with my daughter.

Moe, my mother-in-law who I adore, offered to drive up to the hospital—even though it was 4½ hours away from her. "Call me if you need me," she said.

In the meantime, Matt attended the rally, and after that he went to Indiana for two weeks. He never communicated his travel plans with me.

"Please let me know about your trips ahead of time," I requested.

Matt began to let me know he was going away the day before he left, which made me furious. I felt it was painful and inconsiderate that he didn't tell me in advance anymore. I didn't understand why that was so difficult for him to do.

During all of this chaos, I faithfully went to Zumba class. That was the only stable thing left in my life. Between my marriage issues and Alyssa's new MS diagnosis, I felt like I was falling apart. I had no one to lean on, yet everything was on my shoulders. My girls' dad was out of the state for a month. All of my family lives far away. My trusted, good friends live several states away in Maryland. And it seemed that my husband was doing everything he could to get as far away from me as possible.

It's no wonder I ran to Zumba five days a week. It became my therapy. I felt driven to get healthy.

In May, we hit our marriage breaking point. After a few weeks away, Matt came home for around three days. "I'm leaving for another rally," he said unexpectedly.

"I'll go with you," I said.

"No. Maybe next time," Matt said.

"How long will you be gone?" I asked.

"A few weeks," Matt said.

By then, tears were streaming down my face. "I can't do this anymore," I said. "I'm done! Nothing is improving. Something has to give here. I don't want to be alone all the time. I just mentally processed my daughter having multiple sclerosis at twenty-four years old. Thank God, she will be okay." I felt like I was going to break at any moment. "This is why people get married: So they don't have to be alone. You are my husband, my everything, and my companion in this life. I need you. You really need to figure out what you want to do."

Even after I got that all out, Matt seemed unaffected. "I'm sorry," he said.

"Matt, you are either in this marriage 100 percent, or you are not in it at all," I said. "We can't go on like this. I can't do this anymore."

"I promise I will take the time and think it through," Matt said. "I'll communicate better this time I'm away."

I figured Matt would have plenty of time to think about things while he was on the road. Of course, I packed his suitcase and made sure he had everything that he might need.

As Matt was getting ready to leave, I wiped the tears from my face. He hugged me, kissed my forehead, and said, "We will talk soon. Don't cry. I love you."

"I love you," I said back.

Matt took our precious puppy, Yoona, and the RV and left.

Before the truck had backed out of the driveway, I missed Matt so much it hurt.

He was gone again, and I felt like I couldn't breathe.

At that moment, I had an epiphany. I felt like I lost him. Holding on was getting harder and harder for me. I lost control and broke down. I knew in that moment that I still loved Matt fiercely. We were connected forever through our vows and God. That day was May 22, 2024—the day my entire life changed.

Part Three: The Isolation

Chapter 8

Three days after Matt left, I called him and asked. "Have you thought about anything on your drive?"

"I need more time," he replied.

"Okay," I said. We made small talk about our dog, Yoona, and work.

"I will talk to you later," I said. "I love you."

"I love you too," he replied.

For the next few weeks, I texted Matt often, but he never replied. It seemed really messed up that he couldn't text me back. He could have said, "I need more time." He could have said *anything*. But him saying *nothing* was killing me. I was trying not to despair, which was a challenge considering I didn't know how Matt was or really even *where* he was.

On June 12, I finally sent a more serious text—along the lines of:

Why are you doing this? We are married. Not answering me at all is really making me sick. We have been together for 13 years. Think of everything we have built together and been through. And consider how much we love each other. What did I do to be treated this way? If your silence is your answer, that's not right. I deserve to be told your intentions to my face.

Because of the lack of communication, all I could think were negative thoughts, the D-word, and bad outcomes.

Finally, Matt responded to one of my texts:

I talked to my mom. She told me that we both need more time to process and figure out what we want to do. I'm going out of town for a few weeks again. Wil will bring Yoona home. When I get back from this trip, we'll talk about what to do.

This began the hardest season of my life. Some people would call it a storm. During the next three weeks until Matt got home, I tried to keep busy, but I was crying all the time. Matt and I had never gone through anything that serious.

I began praying on my knees every day. It's times like these when some people really find God. My prayers were so sad back then. I would pray to God, *Please bring my husband back. Why is this happening? I'm in a nightmare. Please, please, Lord give me my husband back. I can't take this anymore.*

I tried to stay optimistic. Deep down I thought Matt would be back home in a few weeks. And I prayed every day.

For weeks, all I knew was that Matt was driving up and down the East Coast and working with Wil. I only figured out where he was by checking social media. I saw he was in New York recording some RV reviews.

For an entire month, I was not involved with any RV reviews. I seriously missed my job. I felt a bit of solace reading our subscribers' comments:

"Where is Andrea?"

"What did you do with her?"

"Free Andrea LOL!!!"

It comforted me to see the love our subscribers have for me. *At least they love me,* I told myself. It truly humbled me that they care about me that much. It touched my heart. I sent countless texts to Matt and didn't get a single reply. It was not like him to go this long without talking to me. I began thinking maybe there was someone else. Why else would my spouse ignore me for almost a month?

I have been a Christian for a long time. Matt was a believer, but not all the way. I don't think he was fully convinced, so I began texting him scriptures on marriage and apologies. I also sent love letters and wedding pictures.

At that point, I began praying three times a day. I remember praying, *God, please reconcile us. Please save Matt. I can't take this pain anymore. I can't go on another day like this.*

The reality of my situation was devastating. No matter what I did, the pain of Matt's absence, the loneliness of being by myself so much, and the uncertainty of our future was always there—like a weight in my heart pressing against my soul. I literally could not do anything without feeling that constant, unrelenting pain.

I thought about Matt all the time. It was like an alarm clock went off in my head every hour. "Oh, hello, it is time to think of your husband again." *Why are we going through this?* I asked myself over and over.

On June 19, 2024, I had my first appointment at a med spa for a HydraFacial. My oldest daughter Kayla is an esthetician in Maryland, and she kept encouraging me to get one. *Why not?* I thought. *I need to relax and do something for myself.*

The very first time I met my esthetician, I felt like she was a friend already. When I entered the room and she said, "Hi, how are you?" I could barely answer her before the tears came. I cried for at least a minute before I could finally calm down. It was so very difficult to control my tears.

I told her a little about what was happening.

"God will reconcile you," she said. "Keep praying. Don't give up hope. Matt's probably going through some sort of midlife crisis. You both will be in my prayers."

She then explained that she had gone through a traumatizing breakup about seven years earlier. It was nice to finally have someone to talk to—someone who understood what I was going through. I was so grateful.

After my session, I really took her advice to pray to heart. I had noticed that the only time the pain was bearable was when I was in prayer. I felt that I needed to be closer to God because being in His presence took some of the pain away.

Why is it that when terrible things happen, we run to God? We want Him to fix everything right away—even if we haven't talked to Him in years, believing that everything will be okay. God is so good that He never leaves us—even if we leave Him. (Hebrews 13:5)

As I crept closer to God, little did I know that He had something else planned for me.

Each time I prayed, I poured my heart out. I would plead with God to reconcile my marriage. I would thank Him for my family. I prayed for strength because I was suffering immensely. I could barely pray without crying.

I prayed quietly in my bedroom because I didn't want my two daughters who lived with me to hear me sobbing. But the reality was they saw me break down already every day.

I had never been so broken before. I was shattered to pieces.

Chapter 9

On June 24, I texted Matt:

It's been 33 days since we have seen or talked to each other. I want you to know this break was good for us. I needed to have my eyes opened. I have taken a lot of things for granted. I always believed that you were meant for me. I'm yours and you are mine. Please don't be anxious about coming home. There will be no arguing, yelling, or crying. Either way we need to talk. I love you.

Matt texted back:

I don't want to argue or fight either. I'm done with that. Please don't talk about what's going on between us. We need to keep it 100 percent professional and get you back filming.

I texted:

I agree. I need to get back to work. Please come home after we record so we can talk.

He replied:

I'm not coming home. We'll talk after we're all done with filming.

That was hard to hear. *Wow! What is he going to say that we can't talk about right away?* I wondered.

By then, it had been an entire month with no contact. Yet Matt and I managed to film. It was very difficult—not to mention very weird—to laugh and smile on the outside when on the inside my life was falling apart. I didn't know where our marriage stood, yet I needed to pretend in our videos that all is well.

I thought those three days of filming might just kill me. Filming with him, not being able to talk, and missing being with him so much was excruciating. After we finished filming, I cried my entire drive home.

Yet Matt seemed fine to me. *How can he not be upset or bothered?* I thought. *We've had almost 14 years together. You would think he would be a mess too.*

Finally on June 27, Matt came home to talk to me. He had also planned to pick up Yoona because he was headed back to Indiana. I had packed my suitcase because I thought I would go with him.

When Matt saw my suitcase, he asked, "What are you doing? You're not going with me."

"Why can't I go?" I asked.

"I need more time to think," Matt said.

By then I was freaking out inside, and I yelled, "I don't know why this is happening! I'm your wife. I'm supposed to go with you." I began crying uncontrollably.

Matt hugged me.

"I love you," I said tearfully. "You are my life, my love, my everything. I'm sorry I took you for granted. I'm so sorry for not spending more time with you."

Then Matt started crying. "It's not all your fault," he said. "I messed up too."

"What do you want to do?" I asked.

"I don't know," Matt said. "I feel lost and confused. I can't express how I feel. I can't explain it. I don't know what's happening to me."

We said tearful goodbyes. By then, I was sick to my stomach. I couldn't believe what was happening. I was in shock. It felt surreal.

"I'll be in touch soon," Matt said, wiping the tears off my face. "You'll come out to Michigan in about two weeks to film. We'll have more time to talk then and hopefully figure things out."

"Do you promise?" I asked hopefully.

"I promise," Matt said.

"Please don't ignore my texts and calls. We're married. We should still be communicating," I said.

"I'll try to do better," Matt said.

Then he was gone again.

That was the last time he was home.

Later that evening, my daughter Kayla and my son-in-law, Joe, asked me to do a devotional with them on the phone.

"Sure," I said, although I had never done one before. I knew they were trying to be supportive and comforting, and I was grateful for anything that might keep my mind busy and give me strength.

My close, immediate family knew I was beyond sorrowful. It was hard for them not to because anytime they asked me about Matt, I would weep. They could tell that talking about him was painful for me, and I usually quickly changed the subject.

On the other hand, my extended family and friends had no idea what was happening. As of this writing, they still don't.

The only things that kept me moderately sane were my daily Zumba classes—where the pulsating music drowned out my thoughts—and my three-times-a-day prayers. I also went to church each Saturday and handled business and banking affairs for our businesses. Frequently, I deep cleaned our house to keep my mind busy.

These things helped a bit, but they only worked for a little while. In time I would crack from the extreme isolation, and the tears would start. I had to keep myself constantly busy.

One day, I went through the entire house, searching for anything and everything that we did not need. I started donating a lot of clothes to Goodwill and the Salvation Army.

I was so grief-stricken I couldn't stop crying. It happened in the shower and when I woke up in the middle of the night. I couldn't listen to music, or that would start a waterworks show. The only music I could listen to was Zumba, reggaetón, and Latin music. Because I didn't understand the words, those songs wouldn't make me cry.

Looking back now, I realize that I was going through a season of loss. I didn't know it at that time, but God was preparing me for what was to come. What felt back then like abandonment was *preparation*. God was slowly working in my heart.

But back to the devo I was doing with Kayla and Joe. They chose one at random from a bible app, and it happened to be about resilience, centered on Joseph's story in the Bible, Genesis 37:45. That story is key to my testimony.

If you're unfamiliar with this story, I will try to sum it up. Joseph was the favored son of Jacob. He was disliked by his brothers. Joseph had dreams about things that would happen, and he could interrupt them from happening or give a warning. One day when the brothers were out attending to the flock, their dad told Joseph to go and check on his brothers. He never came back.

When Joseph's brothers had saw him coming, they wanted to throw him into a pit, but they changed their minds when they saw a slave trader. They sold Joseph to the trader, who took Joseph to Egypt, where he was sold again to Potiphar, an officer of the Pharaoh.

Joseph was well-liked and respected in Potiphar's household, and he learned how to run the household. But then Potiphar's wife tried to seduce Joseph. When Joseph refused her, she told Potiphar that Joseph was trying to sleep with her. Even though Joseph was innocent, Potiphar threw him in prison.

It turned out Joseph was well-liked in prison too, by the inmates and even the warden, who gave Joseph a job working in the prison. One night a man who was the cupbearer for the Pharaoh in jail had a bizarre dream. Even though he didn't know what it meant, he was troubled, and he explained his dream to Joseph.

Joseph explained that the dream meant the cupbearer would get his job back. Joseph reminded him not to forget him when he was favored again in the palace.

A few years later, the Pharaoh had a very crazy dream that upset him. The cupbearer remembered Joseph, who went to the palace. Joseph interrupted the dream and told the Pharaoh there would be a seven-year famine in the land. Because of Joseph's ability, the Pharaoh made him Prime Minister—the highest position in the land. Joseph became favored everywhere he went. God had his hand on Joseph through everything.

As Joseph saw, the famine came and affected everyone, including Joseph's family. After all those years without seeing Joseph, his brothers needed to go to Egypt to get provisions. When they arrived, Joseph recognized them, but they did not recognize him. He asked them to come back again—with their youngest brother who wasn't present.

Then Joseph had his brothers brought to his home for dinner. When he revealed himself to them as his brother, they were terrified, fearing his vengeance. Joseph told them not to be afraid and that he would not hurt them. He told them that he would make sure they had provisions for the famine. The brothers were hugging and crying, and Joseph said, "What you meant for harm, God turned into good."

God sent Joseph to Egypt to save a nation—his divine purpose. If Joseph hadn't been elevated to Prime Minster of Egypt, he would not have access to the food storehouses, and his family would have starved.

In the end, Joseph was reunited with his family. They all moved to Egypt. Joseph trusted in God's plan for his life. He had faith in God all along.

That was my first devotional. It would be far from my last.

After Kayla, Joe, and I finished the devotional, we all prayed on the phone for Matt and me, our marriage, and our family. Today, Kayla and Joe are very involved with their church in Maryland, which was the church that Matt, Kayla, Alyssa, Bella, and I attended when we lived there. Kayla and Joe got all the church staff praying for Matt and me. They were still praying for us nine months later.

Chapter 10

A few days later, on June 30, Kayla texted me to say, "My daily devotion was meant for you. God put it on my heart to send it to you."

It *was* definitely for me. It was titled "You Will See My Goodness," and it read:

The opposition that has come against you is due to the glory I am about to reveal for you and through you. The enemy wants to distract you and make you believe that I will not fulfill my promises. You have stood your ground, but weariness is knocking on your door.

Beloved, don't give up. Though the enemy has attempted to sift your faith and steal from you, I am coming to avenge you. I call you to walk with active faith, to roar your promises with passion and power, to remind yourself that I am a righteous King who never forgets nor turns away from those I love. I call you to resist the temptation to despair, to look with faith-filled expectation instead of doubt-infused predictions.

This is not the time to yield to the temptation to break down and give up. It is time to take up your shield of faith and slice through the darkness with the sword of my word. I'm coming to overturn the plans of the enemy that have been put into motion against you. You will see my goodness.

After I read that, I felt some encouragement. Those words definitely spoke to me.

That Sunday, I went to church for the first time in around two years. The message was all about the power of our words—how words can give life or death. (Proverbs 18:21) I felt to my core that God was telling me to watch what I say. I definitely have learned my lesson. I cringed when I remembered how I would say the D word all the time to my husband in the past year of our struggle. I wish that I could take it all back. I don't want to give that word any power—not even now.

On Monday, July 7th, Kayla sent me another message that a devotion she read was meant for me. I was beginning to believe that God speaks to us through His word, church sermons, and daily devos. No matter how God sends His message, you will know it's for you.

That day, the message was titled "Let Me Lead You," and it read:

Are you willing to release the lesser for the greater? Are you willing to let me lead and guide your life, your every step? Every door that closes is the opportunity to see me do something greater. Even if the enemy has stolen from you release the frustration and find excitement in what I'm about to do. My ability to bless is so much greater than the enemy's ability to steal. Never forget that.

Seasons change at times much quicker and more abruptly than you'd like. I've seen you when your soul has been crushed and you're weighed down with discouragement. But if you would let go of the despair and relinquish the right to be mad, I will show my glory in this situation.

All I ask is that you shake off the discouragement; stop asking why and begin to praise me instead. Declare my sovereignty and remind yourself that nothing you place in my hand will ever go unnoticed. You cannot offer me FAITH and receive a curse in return! Give this situation to me and watch what I will do!

I was deeply moved by that message. It spoke directly to me about my situation.

At that point in my journey, I was crushed. My heart was shattered into tiny little pieces. I was way past broken. Certainly, it didn't help matters that I was not sleeping well. Every night since my husband left, I woke up around 2 or 3 am looking for him. Every night, I would reach my arm out to rub his back, then I'd wake up and remember that he wasn't there. I would sit up in my bed and wonder, *Why is this happening?* I often thought I was dreaming that he left. Then I would sob.

My house was so quiet all the time. My girls were busy, and Matt had taken our dog. It was just me, rattling around in our oversized house, with the brokenness and the intense pain.

But despite the aching loneliness and heart-wrenching sadness, I was starting to see that my struggle was no longer with *why* Matt left and *when* he might be back. My struggle had become about surrendering to the *who*. I realized that I was being transformed by God's nearness. I recognized that God was there with me— even through the unbearable pain. This Bible passage came to my mind, *I am with you. I will strengthen and help you.* (Isaiah 41:10)

Independence Day and then the entire month of July came and went. I ignored the festivities completely. I missed Matt and the fun we used to have during the summer holidays. With deep pangs of loneliness, I even missed my dog whimpering at the loud fireworks. It was just me, heartbreakingly alone and desperately sad.

Every day for weeks, I had texted Matt at least once a day. He didn't reply. But I texted anyway. Sometimes I texted about our relationship or my feelings. Other times I texted about business affairs.

Finally, on July 8, Matt texted back.

He had told me before that I would need to come to Michigan in July. I texted several questions about our schedule for filming. When I didn't get an answer, I bought a plane ticket and flew out there. I figured that if nothing else, I needed to get away from our home, where everything reminded me of him.

During my flight from Florida to Michigan, I was a complete wreck. My flight landed, I took a taxi to my hotel, then settled into my room.

Matt texted me for the first time since he left Florida. He was upset that I bought a ticket. Little did he know I was already in Michigan. Then he texted me to cancel the ticket, get a refund, and rebook for the following Monday.

I replied, "I'm here already. Let's go film."

That's when I learned he was still in Indiana. Once again, I had no idea where he was.

I stayed in Michigan for two days. For those two days, I prayed fervently and cried constantly, but at least it was a relief to be out of our house where I was constantly surrounded by memories of us.

After two excruciating days in Michigan, I flew back home to Florida, where I stayed for about five days. As Matt requested, I had rebooked my next flight for the following Sunday, July 14. Filming was scheduled for Monday, July 15, in Michigan at our corporate headquarters.

In Florida, I did my Zumba every day. I did all our business errands and banking. I cleaned my house before I left. One day while vacuuming, I started to sob for no reason. I was beyond inconsolable.

That is the saddest I have ever been in my entire life—even sadder than in 2015 when I lost my mom to cancer. Losing my mother was extremely difficult, and I grieved and mourned for her for a long time. But what I was going through now was something else. I never felt like this when I divorced my first husband. I missed Matt so much. I felt completely lost without him. I wondered, *How can you go from talking to your wife almost every day for the past fourteen years to nothing?*

As soon as I was done cleaning, I put away the vacuum, then went into my room for my second prayer session that day. It went along the lines of this:

Heavenly Father, I don't know how much longer I can take this pain. I need your strength. I'm so devastated and sick. I ask that you reunite and reconcile us. Please watch over my husband, my children, and our family. Protect and guide them in their lives. In Jesus' name. Amen.

That's a Reader's Digest version because each of my prayer sessions lasted about 20 minutes, as I bawled my eyes out the entire time.

I prayed like that from May to the end of July. Faithfully, three times a day, I would go to battle on my knees.

Chapter 11

On July 9, I texted Matt:

First of all, I'm so grateful that God gave me you. He saw the bigger picture from the first day. You have been my rock from day one. Loving me and the girls unconditionally. Working hard for our family. All that we struggled for. I never got to say thank you. I've been blessed. I mean that from the bottom of my heart. You made me laugh, made me feel special. You understood me better than anyone. The way you loved me. Your commitment and loyalty to me from day 1. I had the time of my life with you. The best memories I have are of you and the girls. We have been everything to each other. Knowing our vulnerabilities, our imperfections, our dreams and our vision for our future. That is love. You are my soulmate.

I'm so sorry for leaving you to deal with all the business dealings. I know it was a lot on your plate. You probably felt so overwhelmed. I left you by yourself to deal with it. How can I ever apologize enough? We are a team. The past two months, my eyes have been open. I'm not even bothered by stress anymore. The space between us is the most painful thing. When I took my wedding vows before God and you, I meant them! For better or for worse, till death do us part.

I don't want you to think you have to fix everything. And you're probably thinking you can't fix this? I'm not asking you to fix it. I'm asking you to meet me halfway.

We have come too far to throw fourteen years away. We haven't even seen a marriage counselor. I know we can overcome this. God will restore our marriage. Don't quit us. And please stop talking to me like I'm a stranger. I AM your wife. I know you better than anyone. I love you with every breath and all of my soul. How will you know unless you try, my love?

I didn't get a response.

On July 14, I flew to Michigan. That day, Matt texted me:

Can you film Thursday?

I texted back:

No. I'm here in Michigan now. Kayla and Joe are visiting Florida on Friday. I told him it will have to be Monday through Thursday. I would fly home Friday morning.

He texted:

I will be in Michigan on Tuesday.

I had Monday all to myself. I exercised in the hotel gym, came back up to my room and prayed, then repeated that cycle a few times.

On July 16, Matt finally arrived in Michigan from Indiana. The plan was for me to meet him at the dealership so we could film. It was the first time I had seen Matt since the end of June.

When I saw Matt, I smiled and asked, "How are you?"

"Busy, busy, busy," he replied.

It hurt so bad to talk like that—like there was a wall between us. My stomach was so nauseated, I felt like throwing up. Feeling the space in between us gave me anxiety.

Matt and I got into a golf cart, and he drove us wordlessly to the first RV to film. Without Matt needing to explain, I knew that we would be batch recording as usual that day, filming four or even five RV reviews.

As we were getting started filming, Matt did his usual intro, then turned the camera to me and said cheerfully, "Let's say hi to Andrea!"

I tried to say hi back. But even though I focused all of my concentration on work and trying to hold my emotions in check, a broken cry started and the tears flowed.

"Take a break for a minute," Matt said, pausing the recording. Then he gestured for me to follow him into the RV, where he hugged me.

"I'm okay now," I said. "Let's finish filming."

We had a long day, reviewing one RV after another. Despite our frayed emotions, Matt and I somehow managed to keep the filming professional. Finally, after we were done for the day, I asked him, "Would you do dinner with me?"

"No. I'm too busy," Matt said.

"Okay, well we do need to talk at some point," I said.

"We'll talk tomorrow," Matt replied. "I'm bringing Yoona to spend the night at your hotel."

We had stopped staying in the same hotels on our work trips. In fact, we hadn't slept in the same bed since May 21.

When Matt came to my hotel room to drop off Yoona, I was very happy to see my baby puppy. Although I felt nervous to see Matt, I tried to talk to him.

"I have to go," he said dismissively.

"Can I have a hug?" I asked, starting to cry.

He hugged me, then quickly backed away. As Matt walked out of my hotel room, closing the door behind him, I wondered, *Who is this? He has always been so loving to me. He used to tell me I was his. That I was everything to him. That I was his world. I don't know where my husband is.*

The next day, we got the rest of our filming done. Afterward, Matt was supposed to come over to my hotel room to talk and pick up Yoona. But he never did.

I had a fitful night's sleep in the overly quiet, lonely hotel room without my husband and even my dog. The next morning, Matt called to apologize. "I fell asleep," he explained.

I wasn't upset because I knew he was probably exhausted with all the traveling going on. That was our last day filming in Michigan, and I was leaving the next morning to go back home. In the late afternoon, Matt came to my hotel room. I let him in.

"Please sit," I said, gesturing toward the chair.

Matt shook his head no.

"Let's talk," I said.

"I can't stay long because I have work to do," Matt said.

"Where are you at with things?" I asked.

"I need more time," he said. "I still didn't know what's going on in my mind."

"Can you explain?" I asked.

"I feel like I'm in a dark place," Matt said, searching for his words. "I feel broken. I need a little more time. I'm trying to figure things out."

"Okay," I said. "Do you still love me?"

"I will always love you," Matt said.

That made me cry more than anything because it sounded so past tense. We hugged for a few minutes.

"How can you not be bothered by all of this?" I asked.

"I'm having a hard time too," Matt said. "Just because I'm not crying doesn't mean I'm not hurting. I immerse myself in work. I got to go."

"When will we talk again?" I asked, feeling my panic mounting at being left again.

"I don't know," Matt said. "Maybe in a few weeks. I will get a hold of you for filming."

After Matt left, I really lost it—becoming completely hysterical. The pain was immeasurable. It was consuming me like a wave crashing over a swimmer. More days of no communication took my breath away. I fell to my knees and prayed, *Is this really happening? I really had thought a reconciliation was on the way.*

I was so broken-hearted. It felt like Matt couldn't stand to even be around me. Every time we had to have these talks, he was always in a rush. They never lasted more than 30 minutes, and this talk was only about 15 minutes. It was very strange. The feeling I got from Matt was that he couldn't get away from me fast enough—almost as if I was appalling to him. It felt like his heart had turned completely cold toward me.

The next morning, I flew home to Florida, feeling desolate. The plane landed at the Tampa airport. I deplaned and hurried to baggage claim to retrieve my luggage. When I spotted the empty carousel, I turned around and went to grab a coffee from the nearby kiosk.

An older lady standing by the counter waiting for her coffee smiled at me. She had a kind face, and I wondered if my obvious anguish had attracted her attention.

"Nice weather we're having," the lady said with a soft smile.

"Mmhmm," I mumbled a reply.

"Where are you coming from?" she asked. "Are you here on vacation?"

"This is home," I said. "I'm back from a work trip." I could barely get the words out. Intensely aware of the sadness the lovely stranger must have seen painted all over my face, I started to crack and could no longer hold the tears at bay. "I'm so sorry for crying," I said, trying to pull myself together. But the reality was, I couldn't help it.

"Could I pray for you?" the lady asked with genuine concern written on her face.

"Yes, please do," I said, fighting to regain my composure. "Thank you."

"Can I give you a hug?" the lady asked as she held out her arms to me.

I nodded and accepted her warm embrace. Thankfully, before the kind gesture made me cry again, the barista handed me my coffee. I wordlessly nodded my thanks to her, then I turned again to the kind lady and repeated, "Thank you, so much."

As I turned away, I felt with certainty that God had put that lady on my path. I needed someone at that moment. I felt so alone, and I was desperate for someone to just hug me. And she did that.

More and more, I was becoming living proof that God will send people to comfort you when you need it. Praise Him! He is good—all the time.

Chapter 12

Very eager to get out of the crowded airport to someplace more private where my tears wouldn't be so conspicuous, I hurried to the airport parking lot, located my red Tesla, and drove home. I was eager to get there because Kayla and Joe were waiting for me for a five-day visit from Maryland.

When I rushed in the door, I was so happy to see them. I talked to them for a few minutes, then went to my room to unpack and pray. I hated to leave Kayla and Joe, but I was thankful that Alyssa and Arabella, who still live at home, were there to entertain them.

Unfortunately, that became the status quo for their entire visit. I was so wiped out and emotionally exhausted that I wasn't myself the whole five days they were there. I couldn't do much with them because I didn't have the energy, and also I didn't want them to see me so sad. I was grateful that my other daughters spent time with Kayla and Joe. I kept excusing myself to go pray. Being in God's presence in prayer was the only time I had any solace from the pain.

Thoughtfully, Kayla brought me the book *Battlefield of the Mind* by Joyce Meyers. I devoured that book in the first two days of their visit, mainly during times I had excused myself to my room. It's all about the power of our words to speak life and death. It also talks about the importance of trying to think positively all the time.

I realized: *That* is something I can do. I began practicing thinking positively instead of negatively.

It was a steep learning curve, but even after the first few days, I found myself not wanting to say anything negative or have that type of energy.

That was a big change for me. I always used to look at the negative, and it had affected my entire life. I was continuously stressed, always imagining all the things that might go wrong first before thinking about the right things.

After I read *Battlefield of the Mind,* I bought more similar books. I really became good at controlling my thoughts. When a negative thought came in, I would think of something positive right away. I stopped saying things like, "I'm tired" or "I hate that." I replaced everything with positivity. I began slowing down and thinking before I spoke. That was a very successful change in my life. It's a learning process, and it takes work, but it was totally worth it.

One day during Kayla's visit, she was hanging out in my bedroom with me, sitting on my sofa bench. We were catching up, and out of the blue, she started breaking down. Tears streamed down her face. "Nothing is the same," she sobbed.

I felt so bad for her. Our house has family photos everywhere, especially in my bedroom, which has many photos of Matt and me. Seeing how upset Kayla was reinforced for me how heartbreaking this situation was for my daughters too. It was affecting our whole family. Matt hadn't been talking to them either.

Although of course I don't like to see my daughters upset, I'm not angry at Matt for that. I think he needed to keep to himself to process whatever he was going through, and he kept himself so busy that he didn't think about us. Also, he was really trying to get Liquified out on the market. I know how much business success means to him. But more and more, I was beginning to believe that Matt was also going through something life-changing.

On July 19, I texted Matt to tell him that Kayla misses him.

He didn't reply.

On July 20, I texted Matt a love letter:

Matthew, do this for me please.

Take a deep breath! Close your eyes. Think back to the very first time we said I love you... I clearly remember where and when. You also told me everything would be different now because of those words. I can still remember the dream I had of marrying you. It was 7 years after that. Not a coincidence!!! God put us together for a reason. First it was just you and me. Look at us now. The Journey!!! Love!!! Memories!!! Businesses!!! We have meant everything to each other. I know God did not bring us this far for no reason. All the trials and hardships we went through. This is the biggest test so far. We are being made humble and stronger for our future. You have never quit anything. In fact, you strive to overcome any challenges. I know you! Our story is not over. Our souls are connected through God, love and our marriage vows. My love, my life...don't quit me.

I got no response.

I pretty much texted Matt every day for the rest of July.

On July 21, I went to church, and the whole sermon was about being consistent in prayer—even if you don't see anything changing. That doesn't mean God isn't working. We know He *is* working. We just can't see it. That's why we walk by faith—not by sight. God hears our prayers, and He is on the other side working for our good and His glory. Keep Praying!

On July 23, I texted Matt:

How much longer will we not speak?

I got no answer.

On July 24, I texted Matt some vacation and wedding photos. I sent some photos of our early times together when we were having so much fun.

No reply.

I continued to go to Zumba, which gave me some welcome relief from my pain. I met a woman there, and we became good friends. We began meeting for lunch. She wasn't into RVing, and she didn't know me from Matt's RV Reviews, which was really good. She was a good listener and encourager—a light in my darkness. I began to confide in her, knowing instinctively that I could trust her.

The morning of July 25, I was on my knees in prayer. That was the day I started to change my prayers. I was learning how to pray differently from the books I was reading, and I started to praise God all the time. Here's an example of the type of prayers I began to say.

Heavenly Father,

I thank you for this day and for my life. I thank you for loving me unconditionally, I pray that you will lead and guide me in all I do to follow you. I praise your holy name!

You are good all the time. Lord, I ask that you restore my marriage to Matthew. I ask that you overwhelm him with your presence, goodness, and love. I pray for his salvation and that someone would speak life into him. Lord, I pray you would put me back in my husband's heart. Remind him that we are one flesh connected through you and our vows. I know you are the God of restoration and the God of promises and covenants. I know the promises you put in my heart. Thank you, Lord, for restoring my marriage.

Lord, I pray you would lead Kayla and Joe to follow you in all things. I pray that you would make your presence known in their lives. Lord, I pray for their safety and that you would give them good health.

I pray over Alyssa for healing for her MS. You are Jehovah Rapha. You are the healer. By your stripes, we are healed. I know you can heal her, and I believe you can. I pray you would make your presence known to her, that she would believe again.

Lord I pray for Bella. I pray you would invade her life with your love, light, and goodness—that she would know you are Lord and that she is loved by you. I pray you would lead and guide her in her decisions. Help her to figure out her career.

Thank you, Lord. I pray this in Jesus' name. Amen!

Of course I pray for all my family too. I'm just summing up how I changed my prayers.

At that time, I began reading the Bible more frequently, and I was learning a lot. I started to recite Bible verses almost every day, especially Bible scriptures about marriage. I began watching encouraging, uplifting sermons on YouTube, such as Joel Osteen, Grace Family Church, and Lighthouse Church.

I was learning that we must thank God in the good and bad of our lives—even when we are in the midst of a storm. Praising God opens up the gates of heaven for blessings. Our Creator wants to hear from us. He wants us to talk to Him.

I began to feel that a silent miracle was happening in my soul. The Holy Spirit works in quiet, subtle ways to change us.

Some of the Bible verses I would speak over my life and also in prayer were:

So they are no longer two, but one flesh. Therefore, what God has joined together, let no one separate.—Matthew 19:6 (NIV)

Therefore a man shall leave his father and his mother and hold fast to his wife, and they shall become one flesh.—Genesis 2:24 (ESV)

Let your wife be a fountain of blessing for you. Rejoice in the wife of your youth.—Proverbs 5:18 (NLT)

Love never gives up, never loses faith, is always hopeful, and endures through every circumstance.—1 Corinthians 13:7 (NLT)

There are many more verses you can pray. These are just some of the ones I memorized and spoke over my life.

As my prayers began to change, I began to see all the things I had done wrong in my marriage and all the mistakes I had made. God was not condemning me. He was showing me the way as a loving father would. I could see how hard my husband worked for our family. I could see how I didn't go with him to dinners or movies all the time back when he had asked. I could see all the things I would say no to because of my own reasons and excuses, such as if I was having kidney pain or if I was too tired.

God showed me that I should have been a better wife. I should not have nagged Matt all the time. He showed me that a lot of times I could be really b****y. I should have cooked for Matt at least a few times a week. I should have told him how amazing he was, how much I appreciated and respected him, and how much he meant to me. I should have done everything with him.

God revealing that all to me at once was a shock. I felt so remorseful, and I wondered, *Will I ever get to make it up to Matt? Will he ever forgive me?*

I continued to text Matt daily through the end of July. Sometimes I texted how proud I was of him and what a great job I thought he was doing with Liquified and our YouTube channel. I often told him how lucky I feel.

He never replied.

I cried four or five times a day, which probably sounds dreadful, but it was better than the nine or ten times a day I cried the first few months after this all began. I had never experienced this magnitude of pain before. Heartbreak is real!

On July 28, I was sitting scrolling through YouTube when a video announcing the new Liquified warehouse popped up in my feed. I was floored! I didn't even know we were *getting* a warehouse. I was so happy that this was happening, but at the same time, I was hurt that Matt hadn't told me about it. I would have encouraged him and been supportive. I clicked "play," but as soon as I saw Matt, I had to turn it off. I couldn't control my feelings. I began to hyperventilate as the tears came on. When I looked at Matt, I was struck with overwhelming grief. Seeing him made me think, *Did I imagine the love we shared?* It was like I never existed. Not only did I miss him so much, but he also didn't tell me anything. Had he forgotten that he was married? That tore me up immensely.

While I felt disrespected, disregarded, and sad, what I *didn't* feel was anger. That was a huge change for me. Things that would have made me mad didn't bother me anymore. Angry feelings didn't cross my mind. After just a short time processing the Liquified news, I felt genuinely happy for our team. I was extremely proud of Matt, Wil, and Jen. Liquified was doing great. And God was slowly changing me.

Chapter 13

At the beginning of August, I realized that I was slowly being altered. My interests were becoming different than they were before. Maybe I was gaining clarity from such a long time apart from Matt, maybe it was all the praying, but suddenly I understood that everything that was happening to me was God's plan for my life. He is in control.

I had been in so much emotional pain for so long, but now that I had the benefit of the passage of time, I could see that the pain wasn't something I had endured purposelessly. The pain was revealing my strength. The pain was exposing areas that needed growth. My pain had a purpose.

At that point, I knew that I had to give all control to God. I had to lay it all down at His feet. At the cross, I needed to surrender. When I prayed on August 3, I told God:

Heavenly Father,
I'm laying my marriage at your feet. I can no longer carry this heavy burden and excruciating pain. I surrender all to you.

August 6 was a very emotional day for me. It had been three weeks since I had seen, talked with, or even texted with Matt.

Fortunately, I was encouraged by my daily bible verse:

God blesses those who patiently endure testing and temptation. Afterward they will receive the crown of life that God has promised to those who love him.–James 1:12 (NLT)

Somehow, I always seemed to read or hear the *exact* message that I needed. *Could this be a coincidence?* I thought. *Is it just my overactive imagination?*

Maybe if it happened once or twice, I could have chalked it up to that. But it happened over and over and over. It was amazing how God spoke to me through scriptures, devos, sermons, synchronicities, and repeated messages. It could not be a coincidence. It could not be my imagination.

The next day, August 7, I texted Matt:

When will we film again?

I knew we were almost out of videos, so I was hopeful he would reply.

He didn't.

I continued to text Matt every day—always about how much I loved and missed him. Sometimes I included a photo to show him what we were up to at home. I usually forwarded him the photos that came up in my "memory feed" every day of us. I thought that because I had to see them, he should too.

I cried a lot that day. It was a really difficult day for me. I was buoyed by this Bible verse:

Jesus looked at them and said, "Humanly speaking, it is impossible. But with God everything is possible."–Matthew 19:26 (NLT)

The hot, sticky month of August was moving like a turtle. My Bible verse on August 9 was:

For God is working in you, giving you the desire and the power to do what pleases him.–Philippians 2:13 (NLT)

That one *really* resonated with me. God was *definitely* working in me. I was slowly changing. I found myself more grateful for everything that I have. And I didn't get stressed anymore by things that would have triggered me before, such as people cutting me off on the road or being rude to me in a store. I felt like I was a different person. When someone cut me off, I would think, *It's all good.* If someone was rude, I would shrug, smile, and say, "No worries." Nothing was shaking me. It was inexplicable.

I was reading my Bible verses religiously daily. My verse on August 11 was:

So humble yourselves under the mighty power of God, and at the right time he will lift you up in honor.–1 Peter 5:6 (NLT)

That day, Matt texted me:

Will you come to Michigan to film 8/13-8/16?

My first thought was, *WOW, I have to go to Michigan in two days?* But that thought was quickly replaced by my excitement to see him. I was hoping for a change this time. He texted to ask me to bring a few important things with me. I texted:

Can we talk in Michigan?

Matt replied:

I have a lot on my plate right now. I'm trying to get this all figured out myself. Come on up, and we will talk about everything and get everything out into the open.

My August 12 Bible verse was:

Dear brothers and sisters, when troubles of any kind come your way, consider it an opportunity for great joy. For you know that when your faith is tested, your endurance has a chance to grow.–James 1:2-3 (NLT)

The next day, I headed to Michigan for filming. Since Kayla and Joe's visit, I had been praising God in both the good *and* the bad times. And I was thanking Him for all the blessings He has given me. I thanked him for the restoration of my marriage—in advance. In fact, I had come to *expect* the restoration of our marriage with faith.

My daily verse was:

We can make our plans, but the LORD determines our steps.– Proverbs 16:9 (NLT)

Well that certainly rang true for me!

As I made my way *back* to Michigan, I wasn't even upset with Matt. It just hurt that he won't communicate with me. I was grateful for that brief text exchange because I understood a bit better how he felt.

After a long but uneventful flight, I arrived in Michigan and Ubered to my hotel. Matt still needed to travel from Indiana.

I texted him:

Please come see me at my hotel when you get in.

He replied:

Take a chill day. We'll record tomorrow.

I texted:

You need to come and talk to me when you get here. You did say you would.

A few hours later, Matt texted:

Meet me at the dealership. We can still knock out a few videos today.

I wasn't expecting that. I ordered an Uber and went to General RV. We continued texting on my ride there. I texted:

Are we still talking today?

I felt so lost and incomplete, wondering, *What am I doing in my life?*

Matt replied:

I'm not having a good day at all. Let's just knock out these videos. I'm on edge.

I texted back:

Please come over later. I'll rub your back.

He replied:

No.

That right there brought tears to my eyes in the Uber. Matt continued:

Please don't give me a hard time.

Finally, the world's slowest Uber driver pulled up to the front of the General RV dealership. I saw Matt in the parking lot next to an RV. It was nice to see him, even though I felt he was acting like I was a stranger now.

As I walked over toward Matt, I picked up a weird vibe. I could feel the tension rolling off of him in waves. *This is new,* I thought. *This is not the Matt I know.* I felt awkward around him. It was clear to me the many months that had gone by without us talking or seeing each other was taking its toll.

Despite stress and awkward feelings all around, Matt and I filmed three videos. I noticed more how patient I'm becoming. Despite the fact that I had been traveling all day, had this shoot thrown at me, and I was dealing with this whole situation and frankly would have liked to be resting at my hotel room with a glass of wine, I was not in a rush. That was something different for the previously type-A, hurry-scurry me.

Even with the painful mess Matt and I were going through, our videos did not suffer. God's hand was on us for sure. When we worked, it was still fun. While the camera was rolling, it seemed like all was well. But as soon as the camera stopped recording, the fun switched off too, and Matt and I became strangers again.

After we were done filming, I ordered my Uber and rode back to my hotel. I barely made it into my room before the breakdown hit. That happened every time I had to film with Matt. I could contain my tears while we were filming and I was with him, but as soon as I was alone, I gave in and my emotions came out.

It was hurtful to be with Matt all day but not be able to touch him or tell him how much I miss him. It was very difficult to see him seem to be only concerned about work.

I fell to my knees in my hotel room and prayed. Even though I was crying so hard my vision blurred I spoke life over my marriage and Matt. I praised God—even in these hard times. I had so much gratitude for all that God had blessed me with. I really believed that the pain, the waiting, and the tears were all shaping me to face my future with new courage and faith. On my knees on that not-terribly-attractive hotel carpet, I resolved to stand firm on my faith and to trust God. He is the God of Restoration.

I thought, *I will continue to pray with fervency. I know God will show his glory in this.*

Early on the morning of August 8, I Ubered back to film again at General. Matt was there already, so we got started right away. We were supposed to talk that day, and I was anxiously anticipating it. The filming went well and fast.

I Ubered once again back to my hotel. Later that evening, Matt came over, and we talked for 15 minutes again.

"I'm in a very dark place," Matt said. "It's difficult to explain. I still need more time."

"The Hershey RV show is a month away," I said. "It would be nice if we could figure things out before that."

"I'll have plenty of time to think," Matt said, nodding. "I'll have it figured out before the show." Then he left as quickly as he arrived.

What can I do? I thought. *I can't force my husband to love me again.*

I understood that Matt needed more time. What was bothering me was that he didn't *seem* to be taking the time to think about *us*. He always said he would, but did he really? I fervently hoped this time would be different.

Chapter 14

I was greeted on August 15 by this devo in an app, which I jotted down in my journal:

Your waiting is not in vain because God is at work! The one who gave you your dreams will also be the one to help those same dreams come true. You see, sometimes God makes us wait on purpose so that He will be glorified by the good that comes. We can't get discouraged by the delays that we give up our purpose entirely. You must trust the process.

He has not placed you in your current troubles, trials, or tribulations to forget about you. He is building His glory. God is glorified with our unlikely circumstances. When it looks like a dead end and there's no hope, that's when God steps in. He waits till there can be no other answer except God. Then you know it's God, and there will be no one else to praise but Him.

I needed to read that.

I flew back to Tampa and settled back into the new normal that I was unhappy to have gotten so accustomed to. Going home without my husband weighed heavily on my heart.

I texted Matt every day for the rest of August. On August 18, I texted him:

Been home for a few days. I'm feeling very emotional from the work trip. I continue my prayers 3 times a day and get back into Zumba 5 days a week.

Then on August 19:

My heart physically hurts. This is getting harder, Matthew.

I attached a photo of us from two years before. Then I texted another photo with "I love you."

No response.

Undaunted, on August 20, I texted him:

Good morning! I'm here for you. If there is anything you need me to do. I'm more than happy to take some of your burden!

I included a photo of Matt and me from a trip a few years before, smiling in front of the RV at Motor Home Specialist in Texas.

No response.

I felt very emotional. It had been almost three months since Matt had been gone. My daily verses inspired me:

The father instantly cried out, "I do believe, but help me overcome my unbelief."–Mark 9:24 (NLT)

Don't be afraid, for I am with you. Don't be discouraged, for I am your God. I will strengthen you and help you. I will hold you up with my victorious right hand.–Isaiah 41:10 (NLT)

The faithful love of the LORD never ends! His mercies never cease. Great is his faithfulness; his mercies begin afresh each morning.– Lamentations 3:22-23 (NLT)

I also went to my women's group at church where they all prayed for me. It humbled me to be the recipient of so much caring. I was very grateful for their kindness and prayers.

The next day when I woke up, I realized that the heart pain was gone. Praise God! I finally had some peace.

My daily verse on August 21 was:

Seek the Kingdom of God above all else, and live righteously, and he will give you everything you need.–Matthew 6:33 (NLT)

It's interesting to me that as I look back at that verse, I didn't seek the kingdom of God yet. But I soon would.

The next day, August 22, might have been the first day in three months that I didn't cry! Not once! Praise God! But I missed Matt so much.

August 23, my daily verse was:

We can rejoice, too, when we run into problems and trials, for we know that they help us develop endurance. And endurance develops strength of character, and character strengthens our confident hope of salvation. And this hope will not lead to disappointment. For we know how dearly God loves us, because he has given us the Holy Spirit to fill our hearts with his love.—Romans 5:3-5 (NLT)

That day, I had to text Matt about some work-related matters regarding deposit receipts and banking info. And for goodness' sake, he had important mail here he needed to pick up. *Does he not understand that life goes on?* I wondered. I also texted:

Please check with me before you buy my airline ticket for the Hershey show.

No response.

I was thinking I would visit Kayla in Maryland before the Hershey RV show. I continued texting:

Please start communicating. It's difficult when I have questions about our businesses.

No response.

Matthew, I love you...And I miss you so much.

No response.

Nine hours later, when there was *still* no response, I texted:

Never mind. I will book my airline ticket to Baltimore. I'll stay there a few days, then drive up to Hershey since it's only 2 hours away. Please book my hotel for Hershey since it's for business.

No response.

On August 24, I texted Matt a photo of me and:

Just in case you forgot me.

Do you know the last time we really talked on the phone was May 23? Isn't that crazy! We are married. I bought my airline ticket for Baltimore.

No response.

Please book my hotel for 9/8 through however long we are staying.

No response.

My devo that day from one of my apps was enlightening, so I summed it up in my journal:

Every marriage has seasons of disappointments, frustrations, and grind. Sometimes we bring it to ourselves with bad choices or careless mistakes. Other times we're blindsided by an unforeseen catastrophe. It's easy to point fingers during those times. It's easy to shut down, stop talking, and internalize bitterness or shame. But these moments when our hearts have been broken and we have thousands of words left unspoken are the very moments that we need to lean into our spouse the most.

Before going to bed that night, I got down on my knees to pray. Even though I had changed my prayers to being more faith- and gratitude-filled, I would still find myself crying. I wasn't sure if it was because I was so grateful to God for how much he has blessed me with or because I was spending a lot of time thinking about everything Matt and I struggled through, including financial struggles, life struggles, and the deaths of my mom and his dad less than a year apart.

Yet looking back, I could see the hand of God on both of us—on both our marriage and our businesses. I could see everything so clearly. It made me feel wretched knowing that I had not always been this grateful to God. I *thought* I was being thankful. But this new level of thankfulness was different—next level. I became so appreciative and grateful for every little thing.

I realized that I would have *nothing* if it weren't for God. I knew that I had missed so many opportunities to be thankful, and I had taken so much for granted. God was pruning me, getting rid of what I didn't need. I was walking through the fire. I wish I knew what was on the other side. But only God knows.

Through those months of isolation as I endured such gnawing loneliness, I felt like parts of me were being slowly chipped away. I didn't notice the changes right away. It was like God was reshaping my character when no one was watching—not even me. He was transforming me when no one else knew what I was going through.

Looking back now, it's shocking to me to watch the videos Matt and I filmed during that dark time. It was unbelievable that Matt and I worked together, laughing and carrying on through the videos, all while we were enduring a painful process. I know now that God broke me so I would be pliable like clay. God is the master potter.

Chapter 15

That night, I awoke in the middle of the night searching for my husband again, moving my arm around and feeling for him. I had an intimate dream that seemed so real I could still see it even after I was awake. I was jolted from sleep, gasping for air. I felt my pillow was wet, soaked from tears. The dream felt so real, so familiar. I remembered so much detail—what I was wearing, where Matt was sitting, what we were doing. I didn't have any memory of that event actually happening, so I wondered if the dream was a premonition of something still to come. I believe that sometimes God puts dreams in your heart before a storm to offer you some preparation.

I laid in bed trying to better understand the dream when I realized I had dreamed that dream before, back in June. I looked at Matt's side of the bed, thinking, *It's been months. He hasn't slept here since May.*

My heart felt deeply sorrowful. After about a week of respite, the heaviness in my heart was back. I was weary from carrying that stone around in my chest day in and day out. I didn't know how much longer I could take it. I closed my eyes and fell back into a fitful sleep.

On August 25, I went to my usual Zumba class. Thank God for those ladies in my class. To this day, they make me laugh, and I always have a good time in Zumba with them. I love how the music is so loud that I can't think. That's why I went five or six times each week. It's an hour of dancing—and not thinking. Zumba and prayer were my two breaks from the otherwise constant ache in my heart.

At this point, my three-times-a-day prayers sometimes stretched to forty-five minutes to an hour. They had become a necessity, my lifeline. I feel empathy for anyone else who has had to go through a heartbreaking season like I have.

After Zumba that day, I texted:

Matt I wish you would talk to me like you used to. I think about you all day every day. My feelings have not changed. It's not so easy to forget you have a husband.

No response.

Then I texted Matt a few hours later:

Please let me know if you have things I should bring with me—if I need to grab anything from Florida for the RV show.

No response.

The next day, I texted:

Matt you look great. Your weight loss is showing. I'm very proud of you for sticking to it. I know it can be challenging.

No response.

I texted him:

I love you. I said things will never go back to the way they were. I'm different. We are both changing. God has his hand on us. I believe that God is growing us for our future. Crazy things are happening in our lives. He will see us through this. We are going through winter in our marriage. Spring will return soon.

On August 27, I texted Matt:

I really hope you are taking some time to think about us. This is not healthy. 14 years of talking to nothing. You told me we would talk before the Hershey show. That you would take time and figure out what you want. I'm holding you to that.

On August 28, I texted Matt:

Matthew, the girls are emotional. They miss you and Yoona. Even your loud voice through the house, your contagious laughter. Nothing is the same and it is felt. You have been their stepdad for almost 13 years. This is tough on the whole family. We love you and miss you so much.

No response.

On August 29, I texted Matt a photo of us that had been taken two years ago while we were on a trip in Roatan, Honduras. I said:

I get these pics on my daily feed every day. Have a great day! I love you.

No response.

I texted him later:

Whatever you think. It's never too late. This is not a dress rehearsal. We only get this one life. Think about that. I love you. I knew when I married you that you were it for me. The one my soul was waiting for. I want you to come jump off mountains with me! To skydive and snorkel in the ocean. I want to do crazy adventurous things with you! I always have. I even learned to play pickleball so I can play with you. I want us to experience life again, together. I'm all in.

No response.

You are my life, my husband, and my heart.

No response.

I had gone weeks now without him texting or saying a word to me. I felt I had been cut out of his life, like I was *nothing*. I know that Matt reads my texts, yet he seemed to only respond when he *wanted*. I really couldn't understand how he could treat me this way. However, I knew he was not intentionally trying to hurt me. He is not a spiteful or bitter person.

The weirdest thing for me was that I was not bitter or angry about that treatment. Actually, I was flabbergasted. It had been going on for four months now, and Matt still was not communicating. In fact, it felt like we were farther apart than ever. I wondered, *Is this supernatural? Was his heart hardened? How can anyone ignore their spouse? Is he processing his feelings?*

What could I do? Not much really. I kept praying faithfully. I continued worshipping and praising God. At my core, I felt that something had to shift soon.

On August 30, my daily devotion was all about the weary asking God for strength.

Each time He said, "My grace is all you need. My power works best in weakness." So now I am glad to boast about my weaknesses, so that the power of Christ can work through me.–2 Corinthians 12:9 (NLT)

I texted Matt:

I hope you're able to watch our videos and smile. I'm still in love with you.

No response.

On August 31, I texted Matt a photo of our family in Disney World in 2016. I also texted him a worship song that I love "In Jesus' Name" by Katy Nichole.

No response.

Another month began without Matt. September 1 was a Sunday, and I went to church for communion. On my drive home, I prayed to God about all the things in my life I was thankful for and asked for marriage restoration and Matt's salvation. I prayed aloud—even crying at some points. I prayed:

God,

You are a God of Restoration and promises. You don't break your word. Your promises are backed by all the honor of your name. I believe your promises for restoration.

Suddenly, I looked up and to the left, and I saw a beautiful rainbow!

I took a photo, printed it out, and put it in my journal.

I have placed my rainbow in the clouds. It is the sign of my covenant with you and with all the earth.–Genesis 9:13 (NLT)

The next day, my daily verse lifted my spirits a bit:

When doubt filled my mind, your comfort gave me renewed hope and cheer.–Psalms 94:19

I texted Matt a photo of me, then one of us from the year before at Saltgrass, which was his favorite steak restaurant:

I miss your snoring that used to keep me up. Are you taking good care of our Yoona? I really hope you are doing great. Take care of our baby.

On September 3, I texted:

Matt I'm leaving for Maryland in two days. I'm leaving for Hershey this Sunday. Please send me the hotel information. Thank you, I guess I will see you soon.

Matt, it would be nice if you could respond to a text. I know you read them. We ARE married and have a business. Please talk to me. It's been three weeks since we talked after filming in Michigan.

No response.

September 4, I simply texted:

I love you....

No response.

September 5, I anxiously packed up and left my home to head to Baltimore. I texted:

I am on the plane headed for Baltimore. I'm thinking of all the things I'lve done that I messed up in our marriage. I could be mean and sarcastic sometimes. I was stressed a lot, which caused me to yell. I know we are not perfect.

I was trying desperately to hold onto the thankfulness that had sustained me for the past few weeks, but God was challenging me by reminding me of my imperfections. It was difficult to remain thankful when all I could see were my mistakes in full Technicolor, just like that rainbow God revealed to me. Looking back on my behavior, I could not believe how I had treated

Matt. Remembering everything that I had done in my marriage made me cringe. I reflected that I would get annoyed when Matt would not listen to me. I was often cynical. Certainly, I was not the easiest person to work with. I complained a lot—especially when Matt took non-important calls while we were filming. I nagged him when he didn't do the things I asked him to do. I could be a b***h.

God was showing me all that I had done wrong, and it was like watching a movie playing in my memory. Tears welled up in my eyes, threatening to spill out. I had been a horrible, ungrateful, impatient, stubborn, selfish person! I was wretched. So regretful and sorry. I was bougie. I had shown greater love to the things of this world than I had been able to show to my husband.

The movie of my marriage misdeeds played on a loop in my brain. As I came to grips with my role in our marriage issues, God was making space in my heart for the changes that I needed to make to become a better person, a better partner. I needed to be more attentive to Matt. I had to show more appreciation and gratitude. I needed to treat him like the love of my life, the soulmate I knew him to be.

God was putting me through the fire of transformation. I was being purified and refined. In those months Matt and I were apart, I was changing. Now I was beginning to see and feel these changes in myself.

But I wondered, *How could Matt know? He's never around me long enough to notice these changes in me.*

Of course, I knew on some level that Matt had contributed also to our marriage issues, but I really didn't give that much thought, I didn't really care. Because of the way God was shaping and molding me, I was unfocused on Matt's past and present behavior. I knew that the only person I can change is myself, so I focused on my faults and mistakes.

The flight to Baltimore felt like an eternity. Who knew planes could fly so slowly? After we landed in Baltimore and I finally got off the plane, I texted Matt:

Matt, I'm so sorry for the way I talked to you. I am horrified at the things I did. How I would treat you. My sarcasm and nagging. Yelling and being bitchy. I should have shown you more respect. These last few years have not been good. I hope you can forgive me one day. I love you with all my heart. I never intended to hurt you.

No response.

I had long learned not to wait around for a text from Matt, so I hurried to grab my rental car. I navigated to my hotel and checked in by late afternoon. As is my usual routine, I unpacked a few things into the hotel dresser and settled into my "home" for the next few days.

Like clockwork, I felt the overwhelming desire to pray, so I knelt and said my afternoon prayers. I've shared so much about praying it's probably surprising to read that before all of this happened, I didn't every day—let alone three times a day.

But now I understand that when God is transforming you, He will draw you closer to Him with His word, prayers, and worship. You won't feel called to connect with God according to the calendar anymore. You won't pray only because it's Sunday. You will feel like you *want* to pray—whenever the time is right.

Part Four: The Waiting

Chapter 16

I was awake bright and early on September 6, eager to see Kayla and Joe and to finally see and talk with Matt again soon. I texted him:

Good morning. Please send me the hotel info for Hershey! Thanks so much. Have a great day my love.

No response.

Kayla had scheduled me a HydraFacial for that day at the spa where she works. I was really looking forward to it because Kayla does such an amazing job. It was always a treat for me when I got to see her for my skin.

After my facial, I took Kayla and Joe out to dinner to a very nice, upscale restaurant called Farmhouse. It was sort of an ironic name! The meal was delicious, but most of all I was happy to spend time with Kayla and Joe. I tried to focus the conversation on them because I didn't want to talk about Matt and me. They were thinking of moving out of their apartment into a house. I was trying to talk them into moving to Florida, but they're not ready for that yet. They always tell me "not yet." They love their Maryland church, church family, and friends. I will continue to hope that one day they will move nearer to me in Florida!

After our delicious dinner, Kayla asked, "Could you come back to our house?"

I really wanted to, but I wasn't feeling up to it. "I need to go back to my hotel and pray," I said.

I was very depressed. As much as I tried to go on with my life, I still carried that heaviness in my heart every day. I could only laugh and joke for a little while before my very limited energy ran out because the pain inside of me was so intense. I kissed Kayla and Joe goodbye and got ready to drive the few blocks back to my hotel. But first, I texted Matt:

Hey, I need the hotel info. I don't want to get to Hershey on Sunday and not have a hotel room.

No response.

Navigating the unfamiliar roads kept my brain focused on a task, but as soon as I walked into my hotel room, I broke down crying. I was back in Maryland where we used to live, but I didn't have my husband with me. We usually came back to Maryland *together* to visit our friends and family. But he wasn't speaking to me. I started to become nervous about how he was going to act toward me at the Hershey RV show. Completely distraught, I got down on my knees and prayed:

Heavenly Father,

I thank you for this day and my life. Thank you for the air that I breathe. I'm grateful for the blood of Jesus and his sacrifice for me. Lord, I need your strength because I am weak. I pray that you will watch over my family and protect them.

Thank you for all that you have blessed me with. Thank you for my husband, Matthew, and for Kayla, Joe, Alyssa, Bella, and Jayden. I'm thankful for our YouTube channel, our subscribers, the Liquified business, and the people who work for us. Everything good comes from you, and I'm grateful for all the blessings. Lord, I pray for your presence in my husband, Matthew's, life. I pray you will overwhelm him with your light and love. I pray for his salvation. I pray for the restoration of our marriage. I believe you will restore our marriage. I pray that you will put me back in my husband's heart. And protect his mind from the enemy in Jesus' name.

Lord, I speak your promises over my marriage. Since they are no longer two but one flesh. Therefore, what God has joined together, let no one separate. [Matthew 19:6]

I speak life and love back into Matthew, our marriage, and myself. Thank you that you hear my prayers. There is no one like you. I praise the name above all names. Thank you, God, that you are faithful, and your love endures forever. You are worthy of all praise, honor, worship, and glory, I look with faith-filled expectation as you told me. I believe you, and I know I will see your glory. Thank you for all you have done for me and what you still will do. In Jesus' name. Amen.

My prayers were normally a little longer, but that night, I was emotionally spent. I felt like a wrung-out dish towel. I was learning that we must be expectant of what we ask for with faith. We also must speak God's promises over our lives and situations.

The next morning, I had a lunch date with Jessica, my very best friend from high school. We met down in Pasadena on the water. Even my best friend in the world didn't know what was going on in my life. Very few people knew because neither Matt nor I wanted anyone to know, because even we didn't know what we were doing.

Jessica and I had a lovely lunch, and we laughed a lot. But still, I kept thinking about Matt. It was so irritating to think about him so much. I don't know why I had to. Thoughts of him kept popping into my head. I could be in the middle of telling a story, and pop, there he would appear in my mind's eye. It was gut-wrenching. Most of the time when that happened, waterworks followed, but that day over lunch, I distracted myself to keep from letting Jessica see me cry.

After a nice visit, I told Jessica, "I have to get going. I need to pack and get ready to drive up to Hershey."

We said our goodbyes, and I drove back to my hotel. I packed my things and settled into bed. I was hoping to get a good night's sleep before the 2½-hour drive to Hershey.

That wasn't happening, so I texted Matt:

Hey, I can record if you need me to on Monday and Tuesday before the show starts. It is my job.

No response.

I tossed and turned most of the night, and when September 8 dawned, I quickly got ready and checked out of the hotel. Before heading up to Hershey for the RV show, I wanted to go to my old church for Sunday service. I love that church. Kayla is on the worship team, and Joe works there as their IT guy.

As soon as I broke the plane of the double doors to the church, Joe greeted me warmly. Then he introduced me to two prayer warriors for the church, people who pray fervently, mostly on their knees. Those people go to battle with their prayers! They had an anointing on them. That's when God anoints people in ministry or elders of the church and calls them to do something in His kingdom.

The prayer warriors led me into a small room of the church, just off of the church's sanctuary. They motioned me to sit on a loveseat with one of them while the other sat across from us in a chair. We all held hands.

"Please share with us what's weighing on your heart," the older of the two ladies said.

I told them what was going on in my marriage. I shared how my husband didn't know what he wanted, and how he wasn't even talking to me.

"You need to surrender all to Jesus," the younger of the two prayer warriors said, nodding her head.

I did that months ago, I thought. *Didn't I do it right? I guess not.*

"Close your eyes," the other prayer warrior said. Then both ladies prayed over me.

"Visualize seeing the cross," one of them said in a rhythmic, soft voice. "Lay your marriage at the foot of the cross."

I did that. I felt a lot of love and warmth—the holy spirit.

"We can see you laughing joyfully," one of the warriors said. "Stop texting him. Let him think about how he feels if you don't text him anymore."

That sounds interesting, I thought. *Patience is not a virtue of mine. I'm no good at waiting.*

"Amen," the prayer warriors prayed in unison, signaling to me that they were done. I hugged them both and said, "I am so very thankful for you. Any prayers for Matt and me would be appreciated."

The prayer warriors promised to pray for Matt and me. In fact, I know that they continue to pray for Matt, me, and our family to this day—along with the entire church staff.

God is amazing in all that He does. In your times of trials and hard seasons, He will put the people you need in your path. We all need encouragement and strength from our community, and I had restricted my community so much that my connection with these prayer warriors and my daughters and their partners had become lifelines to me.

I collected my belongings and my emotions and left the small prayer room to join the congregation in the sanctuary for Sunday service and communion.

After the service was over, I said goodbye to Kayla and Joe and my friends. With great trepidation, I got into my rental car, took a deep breath, and got ready to hit the road, bound for Hershey, Pennsylvania.

But first, I texted Matt:

Hi Matt. I'm headed to Hershey now. Please send me the hotel info.

No response.

I started driving, a little worried about not hearing back—driving with no clear destination in mind. I had to call Wil and ask him for the hotel information.

"I will tell Matt that you need to know," Wil said.

A few hours later, Matt finally texted me back with the hotel information. My text tone chimed just a few minutes before I wheeled into town and needed to know where on earth I was staying.

I replied:

Thanks. If you need my help with anything, let me know.

As I pulled into the hotel parking lot, I saw Matt's truck. I was surprised to see it because our new normal was staying in separate hotels. I walked into the spacious hotel lobby to see Matt standing at the front desk. It took everything I had in me not to run into his arms. I calmly walked up and said, "Hi, how are you?"

"I'm good. Just busy," Matt said.

The hotel staffer gave Matt and me our room key cards.

"I have to go back to the show to set up," Matt said.

"We need to talk later," I said.

"Okay," Matt said. To me, it sounded a little dismissive. I got the impression that his mind and attention were not with me—but rather he was already thinking about the RV show.

With my room card in hand, I took the elevator and schlepped my bags to my room. Once inside the privacy of the room, I had a total meltdown. *It's been a little over a month since I have seen him or talked to him,* I thought. *Why must I fall apart? I lose control every time I see him.*

I think a big reason for my upset was that Matt seemed so unaffected by me. He looked like he was just so busy he didn't even know what to do.

Work is his wife, I realized. The heaviness in my heart ratcheted up a few more tons.

What else could I do but wait? I got on my knees and prayed.

When I was done, I started to unpack and put everything away. I was going to be sequestered in that hotel room whenever I wasn't at the show for an entire week. Having my clothes and toiletries still in my bags— or worse yet, strewn everywhere—would drive me crazy.

At 5:45, I texted Matt:

Come and talk to me. I'm in room 111.

No response.

I texted again:

Hey, what are we doing? Are we going to talk?

No response.

I texted him a video of the church service from last week when Kayla was singing. He used to watch videos that I sent to him. I didn't know if he did that anymore, but I figured it was worth a try.

No response.

I texted:

What time do you want to start filming in the morning?

No response.

Chapter 17

Waking up on September 9 in Hershey, Pennsylvania, where you can practically smell the sweet chocolate in the air, but with my husband who knows where in the hotel felt surreal. My daily devo was enlightening. It said that things happen, and we don't understand why. If we understand everything, there would be no need to trust God. God is good, and He is faithful. We are not to reason but to trust him. He promises:

And we know that in all things God works for the good of those who love him, who have been called according to his purpose.—Romans 8:28 (NIV)

The message I received loud and clear was: Wait patiently for the Lord to reveal what I needed to know. Don't lean on my own understanding—rather lean on Him. And God will direct my path.

I was shocked to receive a text from Matt:

Headed to the show. Standby. I'll text you.

Well, that was a first: He texted to say he would text.

He texted again 30 minutes later:

It's going to be a challenge filming today with everyone setting up. If you are okay with that, come on in.

Feeling more hopeful than I had in months, with a little bit of spring in my step, I headed to the show, grabbing a can of Matt's favorite flavor of Red Bull on the way. The Hershey RV Show is the largest in the country, so when I entered, it took me quite a few minutes to walk to our tent. I found Matt setting up the booth, so I gave him his Red Bull and asked, "Everything good this morning?"

Matt and I walked in companionable silence for a few minutes over to the first RV that we would be reviewing. We got started right away—like the well-oiled machine we were. We were talking and having a good time, almost like the past four months of heartbreak hadn't happened.

With that RV reviewed, we moved on to another.

"You can leave now," Matt said abruptly. "I need to record with Wil."

"Okay," I said. But Kim, who works for Liquified, had mentioned that we were supposed to be going to dinner later as a team. "Are we still eating with the team?"

"Yes," Matt said. "They will text you what time later."

Feeling summarily dismissed, I drove back to my hotel. I took the elevator up to my room and did my afternoon prayers. I restlessly scrolled on my phone, flipped through the channels on the TV, and people-watched out my window until I got so bored that I went to play pickleball at a nearby court. I was getting addicted to pickleball. I started taking lessons back in June 2024. I wanted to learn so I could at least play with Matt, but I actually liked it a lot. I googled where there were pickleball courts in Hershey, and I found one minutes from my hotel. I drove over there and played with some people who arrived right after me.

When my stomach growled, I realized that I hadn't heard anything about dinner yet. Finally, as I was getting back to the hotel, I got a text from another team member telling me to meet in the lobby in 10 minutes. Once all five of us had arrived—Matt, Wil, Wil's sister Cati, and Kim, our Liquified Customer Service Manager, we all hopped in Wil's truck and drove to a local restaurant in Hershey. It wasn't terribly memorable, and I can't even remember the name.

Once we were seated, we talked about our show week. In addition to selling RVs, we were also selling

Liquified at our tent. It was a good thing Kim was there to do this because Matt and I always get wrapped up with seeing our subs and helping with sales.

After dinner was over, we went back to our hotel. I told Matt to come up and talk to me in my room.

About an hour later at 9:30 pm, Matt knocked on my door.

"We need to talk before the show so we will be less odd around each other," I said. "Do you know where you are with all our marriage stuff?"

"Andrea, let's concentrate on the show and get through this week. When it's over on Sunday, we will have time to talk."

"Okay, sure, Matt. You keep telling me this. How can I go on living this way? This is tearing me up. I'm sick of crying every day." I held back from saying what I was thinking, *At least it's only a few times a day now.*

"I'm still not sure what I want to do," Matt said. "I still need time. I feel like I'm messed up in the head."

I sat on the couch, looking at Matt dumbfounded. I didn't even know what that meant. *It's like he doesn't even care,* I thought. "Don't you love me anymore?" I asked.

"I will always love you," Matt responded.

Once again, that made me cry. It sounds so final. I started freaking out a little. "Matt, if you want this to be over, just say it. Months of waiting with no communication and me being alone is too much."

"That's not it," Matt said, seeming genuinely torn up. "I just don't know."

You could have cut the tension in that hotel room with a plastic spork. It was hard to breathe. We both agreed to continue on as if we were still together and all was well. Other than my daughters and Wil and Jen, no one knew that we were staying in separate hotel rooms and that we hadn't lived together in four months.

When Matt stood to leave, I asked, "Can I have a hug?" I squeezed him tight.

Then he left.

No sooner did Matt leave the hotel room did my full-on despair start. I couldn't help it. I miss him so much. *How can anyone survive this pain?* I wondered. I dropped down to my knees, sobbing. I started talking to the Lord:

God, how can I make it through this week? I love him so much. It hurts that we are in separate rooms. I have no one to talk to. I don't have my best friend, my husband, the one I vowed to be with for better or worse.

When I finished my prayers for the night, I changed into my pjs and washed my face. I crawled into the cold, empty, king-size hotel bed. I read the Bible app until I drifted off to sleep.

My September 10th daily devotion was apt:

Evening, and morning, and at noon will I pray, and cry aloud, and He shall hear my voice −*Psalm 55:17 (KJV)*

I have come to believe that when you want to become stronger, you can approach it both spiritually and naturally. Spiritually, you can pray to ask God to help you, and you can read encouraging scriptures and books. Naturally, by which I mean in a practical way, you can gain strength through repetition. For example, you might work out several times a week, walking, swimming, weightlifting, doing yoga, or taking exercise classes. The repetition is key because if you exercise just once, you're not going to reap the rewards. Eventually, the repetition will get you the results you desire.

The *most* powerfully way to gain strength is through God *and* repetition. To gain strength in any area of your life, ask God to show you what you need to do in order to become stronger. Then do it again and again and again.

I started my day with that philosophy. Ironically, I had felt the need to get healthy since January 2024. That's when I started my weight loss journey by going to the gym four or five days a week. I was so faithful about my Zumba classes that if I missed a class, I would feel guilty.

Looking back now, I believe that God had started to prepare me for the struggle ahead way back then. He knew that my physical body needed to be healthy to support my spirit for what I was about to go through. What I was going through now was exercising my spirit. This storm was *the* test of my faith. I could literally feel all the stretching and stirring in my soul. It was unsettling and uncomfortable. I was literally in the crucible. Praise God. He always finds a way to speak to us—especially when we need Him most.

I couldn't linger too long on that devo because I had to get ready for the day. This was the day *before* the start of the RV show, and I needed to head over to film a few videos with Matt. But first, I grabbed my coffee at Starbucks. I can't get my day started without my favorite white mocha with peppermint.

Matt texted:

Grab me some Pepto.

The irony wasn't lost on me. He had a stomachache. Probably caused by me. He seemed to be so stressed around me.

When I got to the show I found Matt in our tent.

Without greeting, he said, "We're only going to film two videos today."

That was good for me. I figured that way I could rest a little before the next five hectic days of the actual show. I absolutely love doing RV shows, but the hours are grueling—8 am to 7 pm. That's a long day for me to be on my feet. But it is totally worth it because I get to meet so many of our wonderful subscribers.

That day, I was quite happy to leave around 2 pm. When I got back to my hotel, I kicked off my sandals and swapped my sundress for workout clothes. I decided to do a little workout at the hotel gym. After I did my forty-five-minute workout, I went back to my room. Then I got on my knees and said my prayers.

I glanced at my cellphone to check the time because we were supposed to have dinner that night at 5:30 with one of our channel sponsors and some other influencers. I had just enough time to get ready and meet everyone in the lobby. We left to go to the restaurant—once again I can't remember the name. I was surprised to see there were at least fifty people at the event, including lots of other YouTube influencers. I walked around and mingled, sad to discover that Matt and I were seated at different tables. He sat with our team, while I sat with other influencers. I felt like I had been voted off the island.

That hit me hard. Clearly, Matt didn't want to be around me. He seemed barely able to tolerate me— and only was because of my influence on our channel and business. It was horribly painful. *What did I do to deserve this type of treatment?* I wondered. I feel like an outsider—like the past five years of working together and growing our channel never happened. My work relationships with other employees for our business were growing more and more awkward. *Did they wonder why I wasn't sitting with the team?* I wondered.

After dinner, we drove back to the hotel. Everyone said hurried goodbyes because it had been a long day. I decided to go to a bar across the street and have a cocktail. Why not? I had two drinks, then retired to my room.

I texted Matt:

Matthew, I really hope you are not doing something messed up and dragging me along. It would be horrible

if you did that to me!!! I would never do that to you. This is different for me! I'm out living my life! But I would never disrespect you like that! I am not even here. But don't worry about me.

Matt replied:

Where r u?

Really? I wasn't even worth the time to text full words? I texted:

I'm fine. Go to bed. I know how to take care of myself! See u tomorrow! I'm not a child.

Matt texted:

Who are you with?

I texted:

No one. Are you crazy??

Matt:

Why are you doing this? Why are you drinking? You're acting like a fool. Why are you at the bar?

I texted:

I'm back in my room.

Matt:

Good night

I texted:

I would appreciate it if you did not call me a fool. I think under the circumstances I'm doing great! You're so obvious at the show and honestly, I don't want to do this with you anymore.

When I said he was "obvious," I meant that he was not acting like my husband—like I was a stranger to him. You must remember that no one knew that we were having marital problems. All of my patient waiting was breaking me into pieces. I texted:

So, figure something out. I will stay here for the sake of our subscribers! I'm done with the way you're treating me. Sorry I can't anymore. Almost 4 months is enough.

No response.

Why does this hurt so bad? The heartache never lets up. I was exhausted from crying, completely spent. I missed my husband so much that it made me physically sick. It was so difficult not to run up to him and hug him tightly. Not being able to show affection was suffocating me. Not being able to talk to him like we used to talk was crushing my spirit.

After showering, I got ready for bed. When I looked in the mirror, I was dismayed to see my eyes looking back at me—sad, puffy, and swollen. I put on my eye cream and headed over to my bed. I went to my knees to say my prayers. I prayed to God to give me the strength to make it through this impossibly long week.

Chapter 18

On September 11, my alarm jolted me awake at 6 am. There was no time to get to Starbucks, so I made myself content with a free cup of coffee from the hotel lobby. I went back up to my hotel room and said my morning prayers, then I got ready for work. As Cati and I had planned the night before, we met in the lobby to drive to the show together.

Thankfully, we had time to stop at Starbucks for my beloved peppermint mocha on the way as well, as a round of caffeinated beverages for the rest of the team. We all would need the energy to power through the eleven-hour day!

I was really excited to get to the show. Cati and I arrived at our tent by 9:00, and the crowd was already tight. All day long, I enjoyed a steady stream of subscribers and well-wishers. Many of them approach me with shyness, especially if they ask to take a selfie with me.

Many people come back to the shows year after year. When they come to say hello, it feels like we are old friends! I say, "Hey! I remember you!"

By about 1 pm, we had a crowd surrounding our tent. It gets a little crazed around there, and Matt and I were trying to talk to people, take pics, and keep the people from blocking the path. It fills my heart with joy to hear people say things like, "We love you!" "You guys are the best." You helped us buy our first RV." "We love Matt's Prime Pooping Position." This goes on all day. The love I received that day from subscribers helped to heal some of the brokenness my heart had been enduring. But of course, it was Matt's love I was missing most.

I knew without talking that Matt shared my gratefulness for each one of our subscribers. Without them, our channel would not be what it is today. We owe all our gratitude to our subscribers. At RV shows, I spend a lot of time talking to them. They make me feel so humble. Usually, Cati or Wil takes pics of Matt and me and the fans.

Thankfully, our tent was busy most of the day, but I found it very awkward when there was no one around because Matt would not talk to me. I felt so invisible. It looked like he was pretending not to notice when people said things to me like, "Andrea, oh my goodness, you lost so much weight!" and "You look gorgeous!" I basked in the kind attention. It made me feel so much better to be *seen*. I had lost forty pounds, and I hadn't been in a video for more than a month, so the change was noticeable. Several people even told Matt, "You'd better hold on to her!" Ha! If only they knew. I replied, "I'm the lucky one."

At least ten times that day, people told us what a cute couple we are. Hearing that felt like a dagger through my heart each time. I tried to smile when I wanted to cry. I couldn't help but notice that Matt wasn't looking at me the way he used to. Really, he wasn't looking at me at all.

Later that afternoon, a couple came to our tent whom I had met in Michigan one year ago. When they came up to say hi, I broke down. I had to walk away because tears were streaming down my face. They walked away with me to give me a hug. I could see the concern in their eyes, so I told them a little about what was going on, not all the details of course.

I had recognized a pattern: It seemed that I could only tell certain people what was going on. I always had the feeling that they were sent to me. The couple huddled around me and prayed for me. I know that was God working through them because He knew I needed support. I was so thankful for them. We still talk every once in a while. They pray for us to this day and give me encouragement

After the show was over, I headed back to the hotel. Then I met Matt, Cati, Will, and Kim for dinner nearby at the very bougie Hershey Hotel to celebrate Kim's birthday. The food was delicious. And I couldn't forget *that* name!

As I prepared to leave, I told Matt, "I'm riding back with you to the hotel."

"Did you have a drink?" he asked. He used to say that I get emotional when I drink.

I followed Matt to his truck. "It is so hard to be around you at the show. You treat me like I'm a stranger," I said. "Didn't we build all of this together? You're ignoring me, not looking at me. It hurts! You are killing me. I can't do this."

"Yes, you can," Matt said. "You're strong."

"*I'm* not strong," I said weakly. "My God gives me strength for everything. How do you just not care about me at all?"

"I don't know," Matt said, with genuine puzzlement in his voice. "I don't understand what's going on in my head."

That was when I really accepted that I was all alone in this marriage. I was the only person trying to save it. I believe that marriage is sacred. I will *not* break my vows. "I love you so much, Matt," I said. "I'm still in love with you."

"I just need more time," he said, really beginning to sound like a broken record to me.

I got out of the truck, walked into the hotel, and rode the elevator back to my hotel room.

I was greeted on September 12 by this daily Bible verse:

Are any of you suffering hardships? You should pray. Are any of you happy? You should sing praises.–James 5:13 (NLT)

The irony was not lost on me.

It was day two of the Hershey RV Show. After saying my morning prayers, I got ready for work. It was starting to feel routine already: Cati and I got to the show and headed to our tent. As soon as we got there, I saw a crowd around the tent already. That's when I knew it was going to be a fun day! The closer it gets to the weekend, the more crowded an RV show gets. Lots of people were happy to see Matt and me, and Wil too. We are all talking to everyone and taking pics. I was writing up Matt's Cash for customers who were interested in buying RVs.

After a few hours had flown by, I finally got the chance to sit down. But it wasn't long before I had to pop back up again.

Matt was acting like I wasn't there again. I felt miserable by his coldness. Who was this guy? I keep telling myself that God is going to restore us. But I was trying to wait patiently, knowing it is in God's perfect timing—not mine.

A sweet couple came by to talk to me. They met us last year at this show. I felt like they were kindred spirits. I walked away from the tent with them for a bit of a breather, and they asked me how long Matt and I were married. That made me very emotional. I started sobbing.

"Please hide me," I said. There were a lot of people around our tent. We walked farther away. I let myself speak freely to them for a few minutes because I felt comfortable and trusted them not to tell anyone. I had been so lonely with no one to talk to, going through all this alone. They are now my good friends, and I still talk to them to this day. Of course, they prayed over me and hugged me. I really needed the comfort of their hugs that day. I felt like God had put them on my path for that reason.

Before I knew it, it was time to go. The days are many hours long at RV shows, but they fly by fast. I headed back to the hotel. Thankfully, everyone was on their own that night for dinner. I went to my room, and no sooner did I get in than the waterworks started. I was hit by an overwhelming rush of pure sorrow. I couldn't believe the pain that I was still going through. My heart ached fiercely.

I dropped down on my knees to pray. Being in the presence of God during prayer always made me feel stronger, loved, and more at peace. After prayer, I headed to the restaurant across the street. I ate a salad and had a martini, then I retired back to my room. I took a shower, then I called Matt. "Please come up and talk to me."

"I'll come up at 10," he said. "I'm uploading a video."

10:15 came and went and no Matt. He ignored my texts or calls, so I went down to the lobby to get a key card for his room. I am his wife after all! I went to his room and opened the door to see that Matt was fast asleep. Well, until he heard the door creak and woke up. I felt so bad.

"What are you doing here?" he asked in what sounded to my hyper-sensitive ears to be an exasperated tone.

"I thought we were going to talk," I said. "But you didn't answer any of my calls or messages. I'm sorry I woke you."

"Thank goodness you woke me up," Matt said. "I needed to finish this video upload. Andrea, I'm tired. We can talk another day."

"Matt, please don't kick me out," I said. "I haven't slept well since you left. Please just hold me for one night. It's been almost five months."

We got into bed, and he held me. Nothing else happened. What was weird was the way he was holding me: It was like nothing bad was happening between us. He went right back to the familiarity that only we would have. I wondered, *How could we be so in sync?* Then my frustration set in, *How could he be so cold to me, then cuddle with me like nothing is going on?*

Matt quickly fell asleep and began snoring a bit. I knew he was exhausted. I felt so relaxed and comfortable, and my heartache subsided while I was in his arms. I was proud of myself that I didn't cry. I fell into a deep sleep.

The next morning, I woke up around 6:20 am. I had to do the walk of shame back to my room. I have never done that in my entire life. It felt awful to have to do it with the man I married.

Part Five: The Desperation

Chapter 19

Friday, September 13, was the midway point of the RV show. My daily verse advised me to:

Wait patiently for the LORD. Be brave and courageous. Yes, wait patiently for the LORD.—Psalms 27:14 (NLT)

I arrived at the show to see that it was very busy already. I loved seeing all the other YouTube influencers and manufacturer sales reps. I smiled, happy to feel like I was a part of something again. Even more subscribers came to talk to us that day. We also sold a lot of Liquified. Our tent was constantly busy with customers and fans stopping by. I was overwhelmed with gratitude for our subscribers, without whom we would not have been able to start Liquified. The day flew by in a blur, and before I knew it, I headed back to the hotel.

When I got to my room, I didn't know why I had to cry. It was like my eyes were holding back the pain all day, and once I could relax all that anguish flowed out of my eyes. I let the tears fall, *Am I grieving?* I wondered. I would have thought the pain would start to let up after a few months. It didn't. I still felt weighed down by it. After my shower and getting into my pjs, I knelt by the bed. I needed to say my prayers to regain some peace. Rather than going out, I decided to stay in and rest because I knew the next day, Saturday, would be the busiest day at the show.

Not surprisingly, Saturday, September 14, started with a huge crowd. As I wound around the paths through the show to our tent, I had no idea what remarkable experience God had in store for me. Around mid-morning, a sub stopped by to say hi and meet us. She asked Matt, "Have you ever thought about writing a book?"

"No," Matt replied rather gruffly. "I'm too busy."

She turned to me, looking so excited to meet me. I hugged her because I hug everyone. The first thing out of her mouth was, "Do *you* want to write a book? I'm a huge fan of you guys! I'm also in the market for an RV. I'm a book publisher, and I think it would be cool for you to do a book about RVing."

Instantly I said, "Yes. I need purpose. I have been praying for purpose, and here you are."

I soon learned that her name is Jennifer, and she became a light on my path. God put her there for a reason. You'll see why soon. We exchanged emails and phone numbers, and she said, "I'll be in touch."

I thought, *Wow, that was super exciting! I might be able to pull this off!*

The rest of the day was insanely busy. By closing time, we all were exhausted from the day. Frankly, I was tired of thinking about my husband all the time. My mind never got a break. Neither did my heart. It ached 24/7.

I think Matt and Wil had a business dinner to attend, so I went back to the hotel on my own. I decided to grab something across the street to eat. I needed to get back and pack up. The next day, Sunday, I would be leaving after the show. I had to get back to Baltimore for my flight that left early Monday morning.

For the past few days, I had not texted or called Matt. We only interacted at the show—and barely even there. He had told me Sunday that we would be talking when it was all over. I looked forward to that, hoping that maybe I would be out of limbo soon. I packed up, ready to check out of the hotel in the morning. I said my prayers and went to bed early.

Sunday, September 15, was finally the last day of the long Hershey RV Show. I was ready to be done. My daily verse gave me a little more energy:

The LORD is good, a strong refuge when trouble comes. He is close to those who trust in him.—Nahum 1:7 (NLT)

When I headed out to the show first thing in the morning, I stopped by the lobby to check out and to check Matt out of his room too. I stashed all of my stuff in the rental car because I was driving back down to Baltimore after the show to catch my flight home tomorrow. I was dreading the 2½-hour drive and flight. After loading my car, I headed to the show.

Normally, Sundays are a little slower at RV shows, especially during football season. That quieter day is eclipsed by the daunting fact that we have to pack up at the end! I nervously remembered that Matt and I were supposed to talk at some point later.

I was momentarily distracted from that by checking our Liquified sales. We were offering a promotion where if we sold out of our Liquified bundle packs, we would make a $10,000 donation to the SPCA of Elkhart. That's the RV capital of at least the United States—if not the world. Most of the RV manufacturers are headquartered there. I was pleased to see that we were very close to selling out! Our customers were so supportive, and some of them bought two bundles.

Most of the day, Matt and I met subs and took selfies with them. It is so surreal talking to so many people all day long. I feel a connection with almost everyone. I could stand in that tent all day and talk to them. People treat Matt and me like we are celebrities. I'm always like, "Nope, we are just like everyone else." We try to stay grounded. Matt and I wanted to create this channel to help consumers determine which RV is best for them. We also wanted to prevent people from being ripped off.

As I watched Matt interact with fans, I was reminded how he has no filter, which is simultaneously a good and bad thing. It's one of the reasons I fell in love with him.

After the last hour of the show, we started packing up to leave. General RV packed and stored our tent and tables.

I headed out of the show and began the long trek back to my car. I had to wait for Matt because I had no idea what his plan for talking was. About forty-five minutes later, he strolled to the lot, hopped into his truck, and texted me the address to my hotel in Baltimore:

We'll talk there. I don't have very long because I have to pick up Yoona in Maryland.

I made it to the hotel before Matt. He had stopped to grab something quick to eat. I checked in and texted him the room number. I was already getting emotional, wondering, *Why is it he never has time to talk to me?* He made me feel like this every time. All these months, we have talked for a total of one hour with the meetings combined. And most of that talk was about work. Saddened beyond belief, I was really trying not to cry.

Then I heard a knock on the door. I let Matt in.

"Please sit down," I said.

Matt sat on the bed. I sat on the chair across from him. We talked about work for a few minutes.

"Did we hit the goal?" I asked.

"Yes, with internet sales," he said.

I felt excited about that. "How are you doing?" I asked.

"I still don't know what I want," he said. "I feel so lost and in the dark."

These are the strangest answers, I thought, wishing Matt had something new to say. "I miss you so much," I said. "I can't do this much longer. I'm holding on by a thread. I'm lonely, and you don't talk to me or communicate with me."

"I'll do better with communication," Matt said.

Those are hollow words, I thought, but I said, "Matt, this is killing me. I have been with you for so long. Then you're gone. The pain is every day. I pray three times a day."

I could see that broke through to Matt. He teared up. "Just because I don't tell you all the time that I'm in pain doesn't mean that I'm not in pain too," he said. "It hurts. It sucks."

"I know," I said. "So why are we still apart?"

"It's a lot of stuff," he said. "Not just us."

"What?" I asked, feeling a glimmer of hope that maybe we were finally getting somewhere.

"I feel like I don't know who I am or what I want to do with my future," Matt said. "We'll talk in a few weeks at the open house in Elkhart." We go to the manufacturer's open house there every year. Matt stood to leave.

"Are you leaving?" I asked. "Every time we talk, you never spend more than fifteen minutes with me."

"I'm busy," Matt protested. "I have a lot of work to do."

"Of course," I said, resigned. "I'll see you later. Drive safely. I love you."

"I love you too," Matt replied. "I'll be in touch."

As soon as Matt was gone, I cried. The entire week was traumatizing. How could anyone take this? I must work with my husband and wrestle with tears all the time. I must smile while he acts like I'm repulsive.

Blinking away my tears, I vowed, *I will not give up. I love him so much. Our wedding vows are inscribed in my heart.*

My soul would not accept that we are at the end. It did not feel over. I said my prayers for the night, then went to bed early. My flight the next morning back to Tampa left at 7 am, so it would be an early wake-up.

Chapter 20

September 16, I was relieved to be flying back to sunny Florida. My flight arrived early, and I drove home. I had a lot to do: mail, banking, business stuff, laundry, appointments, and Zumba. I really needed my Zumba therapy after that week.

I texted Matt:

Please book my flight for 9/19 or 9/20 for Elkhart.

No response.

I had to attend the RV open house. It is put on by all the manufacturers, and it's there that we learn about all the new upcoming year's RV models.

I texted Matt:

Hey, everything is mailed out. I will wait for the checks. Please send me the flight info. Don't forget to book it, I know you are getting sidetracked.

No response.

Seven hours later, I booked my flight myself. The tickets were going so fast that I had to fly into South Bend, Indiana. Clearly, many people from all over the country were attending the open house. I could not wait for Matt to find time to book my ticket.

I texted Matt:

I bought my ticket for Saturday 9/21.

Matt texted:

You should've waited for me to buy it.

I texted:

Well, you didn't respond.

Matt texted:

For business reasons we had new procedures with flights.

I texted:

How would I know if no one tells me these things? I'm sorry. I know now. I won't do that again.

After all my errands were done, I went to Zumba. It was really fun, and I needed it. When I got home, I jumped in the shower. I was so exhausted from being up so early. The fatigue from the show hit me. I could barely keep my eyes open. Of course, I said my prayers.

When I woke on September 17, I thanked God for this day and for my life—as I normally do right when I wake up. I lay in my bed thinking, *Is this really happening to me?* I remembered how Matt used to love me. He would always check on me. We were deep into uncharted territory. I was so sad, and the tears started to fall as I looked at his empty side of the bed, his things around our room, and our pictures hanging everywhere.

I didn't know how anyone could survive this. I was fighting every day to make it—one day at a time, sometimes one minute at a time. How could it be September, and my husband still doesn't know what he wants to do?

Sometimes I thought, *Maybe I should stop fighting for this marriage. I'm the only one fighting, and I'm so tired.*

Yet I ask you: Please do not misjudge or mistreat my husband. He is the most caring, selfless, generous person I know. Through all of this he has not been disrespectful. Marriage is hard. And no marriage is perfect. I would not have written this book if I were bitter or angry. Even before I started writing this, I had already forgiven him. God had been slowly working in me.

At that point, I began to bolster my energy and summon my strength to see Matt again the following weekend at the open house in Indiana. But first, I needed to get all my errands done and do my Zumba for the week. I said my morning prayers. I was still praying obediently three times a day.

My Bible verse on September 18 felt like a turning point:

Create in me a clean heart, O God. Renew a loyal spirit within me.—Psalms 51:10 (NLT)

I was trying so hard to keep myself busy to cope with all the waiting. I had been looking forward to brunch on September 19 with a friend from Zumba. She has been a light on my path. I love her. It is amazing how God will put certain people in your life when you are going through storms. She is so much fun, and she let me know that we needed to dress up for our brunch. I think she loves to dress up, and getting me to do it is a good thing. I had been feeling really bad about myself for a long time. So I obliged, we dressed up, including handbags and beautiful shoes.

We met at a winery restaurant. After we were seated and ordered, my friend asked, "What's new with everything?"

I told her about the Hershey show and what had happened—more like what *hadn't* happened. There really wasn't any change. I sat there with a few tears streaming down my face. "Sometimes I feel like I'm stuck," I said, taking deep breaths to try and regain my composure. "What am I doing with my life? Am I moving forward or backward? Trying to plan anything for the future feels impossible. I'm alone. My girls are grown. I don't want them to see me so sad all the time." After a few minutes, I stopped crying.

My supportive friend reminded me, "God will restore your marriage."

I believe that God put her on my path for encouragement and strength. We ate our delicious brunch. "I'll see you Friday for Zumba," I said. Then after we were done, I headed home.

My life felt so repetitive. Everything revolved around my dedication to prayer, worship, and the Word. That is where I draw my strength. I am weak, but God gives me the strength and grace to get through each day.

On September 21, I caught my morning flight to South Bend, Indiana. I got into South Bend around 1:40 pm. I didn't get a rental car, so I walked outside of the very small airport. They didn't have Uber or Lyft—only old-fashioned taxis.

I don't know why, but for some unfathomable reason I thought Matt would pick me up. Of course, he did not. The year before he had. The disparity, the difference that a year had done to me.

I texted Matt:

I'm here at the airport. I need the hotel info.

He texted me the address, and I hailed a taxi. I couldn't hide my tear-stained face from the taxi driver, who asked me kindly, "Are you okay?"

"Yes," I said. "I'm fine. Thank you." I felt ridiculous that I was so broken that the tears could still find a way out through the cracks. I told the driver where I needed to go, and he started driving. It felt a little fruitless because I had no idea what the plan was for the next few days.

I texted Matt:

I haven't slept well this week. Thank you for the nice hotel. I'm not doing good right now. Maybe I can see Yoona tomorrow?

Matt texted:

Yes, we will be filming tomorrow.

I texted:

Ok.

Matt texted:

Early in the morning.

I texted:

Where? Also, I did not get a rental car so you know.

Matt texted:

It's okay. I'll pick u up.

I texted:

Okay, thanks. Is 8 am good or earlier?

Matt texted:

Perfect.

I texted:

Kiss my stinky puppy! I miss her so much. If you guys grab dinner later, please let me know. Also, for tomorrow can you please try to be positive when we are together? It makes our videos much more entertaining. Thank you.

I finally got to the hotel and checked in. Once in my room, of course, I dropped to my knees by the bed and prayed for strength. I didn't know how I would make it through that trip. The prayers said, I stood and put my things into the dresser and closet. I hopped in the shower because I needed to be rested and energetic for the next day's filming. I took it easy for the night, reading emails and talking to my daughter Bella. I went to bed shortly after I said my nightly prayers.

On September 22, the daily verse read:

For I hold you by your right hand, I, the LORD your God. And I say to you, "Don't be afraid. I am here to help you."–Isaiah 41:13 (NLT)

Before I got ready for filming, I ducked down to the hotel lobby for coffee. Then I returned to my room to say my morning prayers. I saw a text from Matt:

I'll be late picking you up.

It looks like we will be working around 9:30 am instead of 8:00 am, I thought. *That works for me.* I figured I could take my time praying. After my prayers, I noticed I was starting to get rug burns on my knees. Looking back, that feels like both a good thing and a bad thing. After Matt picked me up, we headed over to Thor

Headquarters. Because Thor has a lot of other small manufacturers under their large umbrella company, it seemed like knocking out the bigger fish would be the best way to start. The good thing was that we had five or six motorhomes that we wanted to film.

As soon as Matt and I walked into the display, we were met by some Thor sales reps.

"You look great with your weight loss," one of the reps said with a smile, "You've turned into a power couple!"

"No way," Matt and I said in unison.

That compliment stung a little bit. No one knew how much pain I was in when they said things like that. It wasn't their fault. I was still struggling with the heaviness in my heart. On the inside, all I could think was, *How does he do this?*

After we were done with that very long day of recording, Matt dropped me off at my hotel, then went to get Yoona for me to watch while he recorded with Wil. It doesn't make any sense to me why he didn't take me with him while he grabbed her. About thirty minutes later, Matt called to say, "Come outside and grab her."

When I saw Yoona, she looked so happy. She ran up to me, smiling and wagging her butt. My dog loves to twerk. Yoona is so cute, and whenever she is excited, she shakes her booty, and her eyes get squinty.

"Bye," I said to Matt. "See you in a few hours."

I turned away from him and went back to my hotel room. As soon as Yoona and I got in, I could not hold in the tears. Wrecked by tears, I could hardly breathe. Poor Yoona was worried. She was trying desperately to get in my face, which she was easily able to do because I was already on the floor to pray.

Heavenly Father,

Thank you for my life, the air that I breathe. Lord, I need your strength. I am weak, and this pain is unbearable. It is crushing me.

There is no one like you. I praise your holy name, the name above all names. Thank you for blessing me with my husband, daughters, family, and friends. Thank you for our YouTube channel, our subscribers, and the Liquified business. Everything good comes from you.

I humbly ask for forgiveness of my sins—that you would help me to be a better Christian, wife, and mother. Please protect and guide my children. Please guide and protect my parents and siblings. I pray for my mother-in-law, that her health is good and that she is safe.

I pray for salvation for my husband, Lord, that you would overwhelm his life with your love, light, presence, and goodness. I know that you work all things together for the good. I believe you will restore and reconcile our marriage. Please lead and guide me in all I do to follow you. Use me to be a vessel for your kingdom, for your glory.

I pray for protection over Matthew, our marriage, and commitment to each other, and over Kayla, Joe, Alyssa, Bella, and Jayden from the enemy. In Jesus' name, you are God almighty, all-powerful, I look to you with faith-filled expectation for marriage restoration. I pray that you will put me back in my husband's heart. We are one flesh. Since there are no longer two but one, let no one split apart what God has joined together.—Matthew 19:6 (NLT)

Thank you that your love endures forever, and you are good all the time. I speak life and love into my life, my husband's life, and our marriage. Thank you for hearing my prayers. Thank you for the restoration of our marriage. You are worthy of all honor, all glory, and all praise. I pray this in the matchless name of Jesus. Amen.

After saying my prayers, I get up to wipe my face. My prayers were not long that time. I figured I could pray longer after Yoona was gone. I felt a lot better after that.

September 23 would be my last day filming at the open house. It seemed my husband had already bought me a ticket to fly back home first thing in the morning the following day—without even asking what time I wanted to leave. *He must want me out of here*, I thought.

I did my morning prayers and got ready for work. Then I texted Matt to see when he was picking me up for filming. He said thirty minutes.

I was excited that we were going to one of my favorite manufacturers today—Nexus. I love the way they treat their customers, and their RVs are great quality as well. After Matt picked me up, we headed over to Nexus to film two videos. We also got to meet some RV owners, which I always love.

After we were done, Matt said, "I'm done filming the open house with you. I'm going to film towables with Wil." He took me back to my hotel around noon.

Before I got out of the truck, I asked Matt, "How are you doing? I thought we were going to try to communicate more and take small steps. It seems like you are so busy you've forgotten what you said to me. I can't take this anymore. I'm living in a nightmare."

"I don't know," Matt replied with a haggard look on his face. "I'm confused. I need more time."

He always says he needs more time, I thought. Waiting for him to figure out what he wanted was excruciating. I tried to fight back tears. Every time I had to say goodbye to Matt, I went through the breaking process all over again. As I got out of his truck I said, "I love you."

"I love you," Matt said. "I'll be in touch."

"Will you please answer my texts and not ignore me?" I asked. "It's rough when you do that to me."

"I promise I will not do that anymore," Matt said.

After Matt drove away, I felt bad talking to him about our marriage issues because I knew he had to film. I didn't want him to be in a bad mood because I brought up our problems, so I texted him:

I'm so sorry. I didn't want to talk about it. I really tried. I love you! I just pray for the day that you call me baby again.

No response.

Later around 6:30 pm I texted:

Hey, I never flew out of South Bend. How is security. It's not long right? Just trying to figure out when to get

to the airport. It's like 45 min from here. I hope I can get an Uber that early.

No response.

Please don't ignore me. You told me today that you would not do that anymore. I just thought you would know about security because you have flown out of South Bend.

No response.

As I was leaving for Tampa at the crack of dawn the next day, I texted Matt:

Good thing you got this ticket for early this week. Florida has a hurricane watch right now. I'm not going to talk to you for the rest of the week. I'm trying to give you space. Baby steps. See you when you get back. It will be a good time at our rally. Just don't go back to ignoring me. It's brutal.

Of course, our Matt's RV Reviews rally was cancelled due to the back-to-back hurricanes, so that was another missed opportunity to connect with Matt.

Part Six: The Deliverance

Chapter 21

I arrived safely in Tampa, ahead of the hurricanes. I got home, unpacked, and went through the mail, sighing with a heavy heart, thinking, *This is killing me. I don't know how much longer I can carry on with this solitude and suffering.* Leaving Matt after work trips was not getting any easier. But what made me feel more desperate was I never knew when I would see Matt or talk to him again.

I hope that no one ever has to go through something like this. I am aware everyone has their own unique testimony. We all go through tough seasons and storms in our lives. I was learning that when those things happen, it's usually because God is trying to teach us or transform us.

Before I got ready for bed, I said my nightly prayers. I cried to sleep that night. It had been 139 days since Matt left me. I wanted to pack a suitcase and just go to the airport—with no planned destination. I felt irrational, but I really didn't care. Maybe I needed to be irrational. After all, *I* wasn't the one who left home. *I* wasn't the one who ran away. Despite a few moments fantasizing about skipping town, I knew that I would never do that. Too many people need me.

On September 25, I forced myself to go to my 10:30 am Zumba class. I just wasn't feeling it. I felt crushed by the constant pain and exhausted from lugging around this heartbreak all day every day. I felt so cut out of

Matt's life, it was like I wasn't on planet Earth with him anymore.

I got to my knees, sobbing with tears flowing down my face. After a few minutes, my T-shirt was soaked with tears. I prayed.

God, please have mercy on me. I beg you, my Sovereign Lord. I can no longer bear this anymore. This is profoundly the most severe pain. My heart throbs and aches to no end. Why do I have to love my husband so fiercely? Take this pain from me, please.

Lord, have I not been an obedient daughter? I have prayed three times a day on my knees straight for 140 days. Prayer has become a necessity for me. I worship and praise your name. I am seeking you day and night in your word. I only listen to worship music. Please take this from me.

Lord, you are good all the time. I can do nothing without you. You know you are the beat in my heart. Hear my cries. Thank you, that you are faithful and your love endures forever. I'm grateful you hear my prayers. I pray this in the precious name of Jesus. Amen.

On September 26 when I woke up, I gave my usual silent prayer of thanks: *Lord, thank you for this day and my life.*

Then I got up and got coffee. I said my morning prayers.

After that, I felt better. I paused to check in with my body and discovered that my heart wasn't hurting. The heaviness was gone. It was strange. I felt at peace.

I looked around my bedroom and thought, *Is this real? Am I imagining this feeling?*

My anxiety, sadness, and heart pain were GONE!

This was really weird. I felt pretty good—the best I had felt since Matt left home on May 22.

I looked around my bedroom at pictures of Matt and me. So far so good. No tears or sadness. Praise God!

The calm that I felt came from deep within me. It felt like a wash of peace had flowed over me. That entire day, I noticed incidents that normally would have caused me anxiety or sadness had no effect on me.

It felt like a miracle.

I went to Zumba around 5:00 pm—more than a little ecstatic to go to the gym. The Latin music further raised my vibration. I was vibing high now!

That night before bed, I said my prayers.

God, thank you, for that I didn't have any heartbreak pain all day.

And that is what I called it in my prayers going forward: heartbreak pain.

The next morning, I woke up thanking the Lord for the day and my life. I noticed that I felt the same calm. Praise God! I had an appointment with my aesthetician that day, and I could hardly wait to tell her!

Could this just be temporary? I thought. *That makes me sad. I'm going to enjoy it however long it's here for.*

After my coffee run to Starbucks, I came back home and said my morning prayers. I thanked God for taking the pain away. What other explanation was there? It had to be Him. This calm that I had was not of this world. I got dressed to go to my appointment.

As I was driving, someone cut me off and almost hit me. I surprised myself by thinking, *No worries!* I literally didn't care—whereas in the past, as recently as the day before, that would have triggered me to spiral into upset and anxiety.

For the first time in a long time, I felt *excited*. When I got to the med spa, I hugged my aesthetician.

She pulled back to see my face and said, "You look good. You're glowing."

At that point, I had only known her for a few months, but she was already a light and friend to me. She is so encouraging and knows what I'm going through. There are not many people I could talk to. I filled her in on my Indiana work trip and how Matt and I did not really talk about our marriage or our future. I told her he said that he needed more time, that he was confused. I said I was so sad when I got home that I literally thought

I would break. I had enough. I told her how I begged God for mercy, to take this pain out of my heart. And he did. Praise God!

"I have this peace in me," I said. "The heartbreak pain is gone."

"That is the peace that transcends all understanding [Philippians 4:6-7]," she said. "The same thing happened to me when I got to my breaking point." As my friend expertly smoothed and soothed my skin, she asked, "Have you prayed for God's will to be done in your life?"

"No," I said.

"Make sure you do that. And seek the Kingdom of God first," she said. "You should also pray for what your divine purpose is."

"What's that?" I asked.

"Everyone has a divine purpose," she said. "Sometimes we don't heed the call when God calls us. Other times, we just don't know what it is that you feel a pull to. Sometimes God can put it in a dream or speak it to your heart."

I made a mental note to start praying for these things. I had been feeling like I wanted to do more for the kingdom, but I didn't know what to do. I signed up at church to volunteer. I love to make donations and do charity work. I was sure there was more I could help with.

After my session was over, feeling calm and renewed, I said, "Thank you. I am grateful you're in my life. I know you were meant to be on my path. See you next month."

When I got home, I said my afternoon prayers. After that to keep myself busy, I decided it was time for another clean up. But first I texted Matt:

Hey. What do you want me to do with these 3 boxes of Gary Vee books? Let me know because I'm getting rid of things.

No response.

Please call me so I know what's going on.

No response.

Matt, I want Yoona home. This is crazy. You can't avoid this forever. If you want to move out, it's fine. We can figure out what to do with the house. I miss Yoona, and so do the girls. You can still go to all the RV shows to get away from your marriage. I have to move on with or without you. I've been very patient. It would be different if you put in a little effort. You did promise not to ignore me anymore. This is enough. When it comes to work, I will be all business. There are going to be a lot of things to discuss. I'm sorry, you are not the Matt I married. You left more than 130 days ago. It's clear you don't want me anymore and you definitely don't love me. Looks like it's over! I've been fighting for us all this time.

No response.

I immediately wished that I hadn't sent that text. Even though I felt calm and at peace, I still needed to know what direction my life was going in. I felt like I had no direction. Yet I struggled to explain why I continued to put up with it. I felt in my heart that it wasn't really over between us. I also felt God's presence telling me not to quit. And when I took my vows, I meant them—for better or for worse.

As September came to a close, I called Matt. No answer. I was calling about business, so it made me a little angry that he didn't pick up. I needed an answer. I tried several times and still no answer. So I texted Matt:

I was calling you because of our auto insurance. Since you have new insurance, we should cancel this one. But they won't do it until they speak to you. I will

send you the number and policy. You need to call, or we will be paying for insurance we don't need.

No response.

By October 1, the last time I had talked to Matt was in Indiana. Yet it wasn't bothering me as much as it had been. I felt more at peace. But I did still miss Matt, and I still thought about him a lot.

The peace of God that surpasses all understanding (Philippians 4:6-7): I was so thankful to God that I had it now. I hadn't been crying or feeling the heartbreak pain at all anymore. I was able to focus on doing things around my home that needed to be done, such as house projects and boxing things up to donate.

That day during my afternoon prayer, I prayed fervently to the Lord that His will be done in my life—not *my* will, *His*. I also prayed that God would reveal my divine purpose in life. I remembered to pray to seek the kingdom of God first and above all else and to live righteously, knowing that He will give [me] everything [I] need. (Matthew 6:33) I was now incorporating those new prayers into my daily prayers, and my prayers continued to give me strength to face each day. I'm so grateful to God for all He has done for me.

After I finished praying, I looked at my watch: 11:11 am, *That's strange,* I thought. I was seeing the number 1 a lot lately. Later that day, when I looked at my watch for the second time, it said 1:11 pm. Because that happened twice, I decided to Google it. I read that 11:11 is full of love, synchronicity, and positivity. It is also believed to be a sign that my thoughts are manifesting rapidly—so I should concentrate on what I truly desire. Plus, it's considered a significant time and a sign of divine guidance and connection to the universe. That last one seemed most attuned with my situation, *That's enthralling,* I mused.

October 8 was the first time I had texted Matt since the end of September. I honestly wasn't feeling that upset anymore. I truly believe God had taken that pain away. I was heartbreak-pain free.

That day, I watched one of our YouTube videos. Matt and I were laughing and being silly, genuinely having fun in the video. How do we do that? Why can we still work together? I love my job, and I wondered when we'd film again. I missed it. I thought Matt was still in Indiana, working at our warehouse and getting everything up and running. But who was I kidding? I never really knew anything about where he was or what he was doing.

I texted Matt the Billie Eilish song "Birds of a Feather." I had graduated from listening only to foreign-speaking songs and hymns to actual current music without crying. But that song did make me tear up a little because it reminded me how I felt about Matt.

Chapter 22

On October 8, Hurricane Helene hit in Florida. I sent Matt a video of me telling him how much I wished he was home, texting:

This reminds me of the hurricane in Virginia we were in.

That hurricane was in 2011. Was it Irene? I can't remember. Matt and I were traveling for work in Alexandria, Virginia. Our hotel wasn't far from the local pubs, and we went to a hurricane party at one of them. It was cool to be around people who were fearlessly living life. Matt and I hung out at a little pub and even played outside in the rain. We were not in any danger—just a lot of wind and rain.

I couldn't believe how many people were outside, having a great time in the storm. Everyone was soaked. It was a once-in-a-lifetime experience. When it got very late, Matt and I left, cracking up laughing the whole walk back to our hotel. The power was out, so we had to navigate to our room with only emergency lighting. How can I forget those amazing memories of such love and closeness? Matt and I were bonded together even back then. That night we laughed into the early hours of morning.

Late in the evening of October 10, the day after Hurricane Helene, my home lost power. I was dismayed, dreading dragging my generator out of the garage. I bought it several years before—in case the power went out. But that was the first time I needed to use it. Thank

God, I had recorded my electrician hooking it up so I could refresh my memory on how to do it.

I went outside to assess the damages. Part of my fence was gone. My screened lanai was ripped up in many places. But my main concern was getting that generator going. I felt pretty tired and weak, so I went to Wawa to get a coffee first. Wow that place was crazy with a line snaking out the door. After satiating my coffee craving, I went home and got the generator started. I was very proud of myself for doing that all alone!

I texted Matt about the minor damages so he knew all was well.

No response.

After I got all my phone calls done to schedule the necessary repairs, I cleaned up the yard debris. Then I decided to relax and listen to a devo about Joseph. It talked about how he waited *years* for his purpose to be revealed—and even longer for his family to be restored. After listening to that one, I listened to a few more with the Joseph theme. I didn't know why I kept hearing about Joseph on YouTube and reading about him in the bible app.

On October 11, my daily verse read:

Commit your actions to the LORD, and your plans will succeed.—Proverbs 16:3 (NLT)

I texted Matt a long message:

Everyone is gone. Jayden's family went to the Philippines. Alyssa is over there watching their dogs for a couple of weeks. Bella is also with her. I'm sad. I'm not supposed to be alone every day of my life. It's why we marry. I am literally ALONE. Kids are gone. And they are not kids anymore. We are supposed to be together, living our lives, making memories, and enjoying it. Life is short, and it's a gift. I don't know what you're doing. I feel like you did something really messed up, and you're keeping it from everyone. I pray that I am wrong. Whatever it is. I love you unconditionally! Nothing you've done will change that. The more you

keep us apart, the worse it gets. The pain and stress it puts us through. You know me. Everything about me. Like I know you. I'm not going to judge or nag you. I'm going to be understanding and supportive. In my walk with Jesus it's about putting God first, forgiveness, and loving everyone and being selfless. That's how I feel about everything. Matthew, the past is gone. I live for today. And God willing tomorrow. Marriage is sacred. So is our bond. I know you feel our connection! I am your wife. Your other half. Your soulmate. Your best friend. 14 years of loving each other. I'm vulnerable to you, like you are to me. It's a beautiful trust to have. I will continue to pray for you.

No response.

Then I texted him a picture of us in Texas.

No response.

I purchased a daily devotional called Strength for Each Day. Many of the entries spoke to my heart. The next day, my daily devo read:

When you ask God for something you need, be sure that you purpose to receive it by faith. Faith is the substance of things we hope for, and it is the evidence of things we do not see (Hebrews 11:1). First, we receive by faith, and then, at the right time, we receive the manifestation of our faith. We may wait a short time or a long time, but at the perfect time, we will see in the natural realm what we have already seen by faith.

We must pray with expectation and gratitude.

I texted Matt:

Matt, God has blessed our life together. I pray you will wake up and see it. From the beginning of it, God had a plan for us. Marriages must go through these tough times or else they won't get stronger and make it through difficult trials. We are both being tested right now. It's almost over. Be strong and pray.

No response.

Later that night. I filmed a video of myself talking to Matt about deciding what he wanted to do. I was really sad in that video. I told him I didn't want to be alone anymore. This was becoming way too much for me.

I sent the video to Matt, but I regretted sending it immediately after.

I also texted him:

Don't give in to temptation. I'm fighting just like you. I'm faithful and loyal to you. Do the same for me.

No response.

On October 13, I texted Matt a bunch of photos of our family and said:

Look how much we loved each other. You are a huge part of the girls' lives. They see you as their stepdad. You are our family. Look how long you have been in their lives. They are hurt. They asked me what they did that you won't talk to them. We all love you.

No response.

My daily verse on October 14 read:

"For I know the plans I have for you," says the Lord. "They are plans for good and not for disaster, to give you a future and a hope."–Jeremiah 29:11 (NLT)

Those words brought me comfort. I sure was tired of waiting, but it gave me peace to be reminded that God has a plan.

The next day's verse read:

The LORD is close to the brokenhearted; he rescues those whose spirits are crushed.–Psalms 34:18 (NLT)

That one sure resonated with me. I texted Matt:

Hi, my Husband ☺ hope you're doing good. Something told me to text you. Just wanted to say I love you way past forever!

No response.

So basically, we had no communication. The last time Matt had communicated with me was when I left him in Indiana on September 24. It had been almost a month.

On October 17, I texted Matt some business questions.

No response.

A few hours later, I texted:

Hi! Yoona is due for her flea meds, which I have. She also needs to go to the vet by November. She is due for her heartworm shot. The shot is every 6 months. We took her the last time. Give her a kiss for me.

No response.

Little did I know that Matt had been in Indiana that whole time. I thought he would be coming back to Florida after the open house was over.

I texted Matt:

Matt you look so handsome! I gotta say you are looking amazing! Your weight loss is really showing. Proud of you.

No response.

On October 18, my daily devo from Strength for Each Day read:

If we want to succeed at what we do, it is vital that we invite God to be in charge of the project. Whether we are trying to build a marriage, a business, or a life, our labor will be in vain unless God is the head of the building committee. God is waiting to be invited to help you, and all you need to do is ask Him. Humble yourself under His hand, and He will guide and direct you.

I texted Matt:

Hi! Just wanted to make sure you're okay? I meant that! I'm here for you always! For better for worse.

No response.

These days, I was positive most of the time. I felt a lot more confident. I still had the peace of God, which made me calm. I still regretted texting Matt that last video. It was a mistake. I think I was just lonely and missing him.

Chapter 23

Looking back, I call October 19 Doomsday. I got up, thanked the Lord for the day and my life, and grabbed my coffee. I came back home and said my morning prayers. Then I checked emails. I immediately saw a message from Matt. Typing this made me cry.

Hey Andrea,

I hope this message finds you well. I've been doing a lot of thinking lately, and after spending the last six months apart, I believe it's time for us to have an honest conversation about our relationship.

First and foremost, I want to apologize for being a coward and sending this in an email. After careful consideration, I feel that it would be best for us to move forward with a divorce. This decision has not come lightly, and I want to acknowledge the time we've spent together and the memories we created.

I believe it's important for us to discuss this in person when you feel ready. I'll be back in Florida early November, and we can have this conversation then. I want to approach this situation with respect and understanding for both of us.

Matt Foxcroft

OMG! I was livid. How can anyone send an email to their wife of fourteen years asking for a divorce? This practically killed me. There are no words to describe how I felt. It felt like betrayal. I trusted him with my heart. I could not believe Matt emailed me like this. I knew that video I sent would get a reaction. *It's all my fault.*

I tried to call but no answer. Big surprise there. I responded with an email back.

Matt,

We need to talk. Call me. I will not yell or cry. I promise. I don't do that anymore. This is not the right thing for us to do.

And I don't want to wait a few weeks. It's been half a year. And you drop this on me in an email. It's a little much. Fourteen years. We don't quit because of struggles. This separation has changed us for the better. We are going to be stronger and closer. You must give us a chance to work. We are meant to do so much more. God did not make a mistake. All my life led up to you. Even the way it happened. God will turn everything into his glory. Open your heart for things that you think are impossible, will happen. I know we are meant to be together. I have seen dreams of us in the future. Don't give in to the negativity and the enemy who comes to steal, kill, and destroy. I pray for you every day. I believed this whole time that God would restore us! And He will!

I love you. You need to stop and realize that this is not who you are.

Your wife,

Andrea

I got on my knees and prayed. I was tearful, but I remained faithful and confident—despite what just transpired.

Heavenly Father,

My Lord, My God, I don't believe what is happening. I know you are the God of Restoration. I know that you are faithful. You told me that when it looks like it's the end, that's when you will reveal your glory. I believe in your promises and your Word. The enemy is not going to make me quit. I look with faith-filled expectation for my marriage restoration. I know that there is nothing impossible for you. I know you will reveal your glory in this situation. Thank you that you hear my prayers. You are good all the time, and your love endures forever. In Jesus' name I pray. Amen.

After that prayer, I pulled myself together.

I texted Matt:

Hey, I cannot understand why you would email me like that. You don't know who I am. I am ready to have a conversation with you. I'm not going to give you a divorce. So much has changed, and you have not given us a chance, especially after going through so much. Do not quit because you feel like it's difficult. You are a fighter! And we are meant to do more. Right now, I'm not crying because I know that God wants us to work through this. Talk to me. I will not cry or yell. In half a year, we have grown. I know you. And this is not what is meant for us. Fourteen years is not something to quit. Marriages have gone through worse. A year of struggle does not define us. Please stop addressing our marriage like a business. It's a marriage. And we both had to change for what is coming. And it is all going to be amazing. You don't realize the faith I have.

I texted him our wedding picture and said:

Remember this! And our vows. We still love each other like this. It's about growing back together in our changes. If you still have love for me, don't do this. You have given us no time together. In the last six months, we haven't taken any time to spend with each other. Give that a chance before you quit. We are not quitters. Matthew, I would speak life and love into you. Our marriage is still alive. Give us the chance that you didn't. You don't even know what I've been doing or how much I have changed. Only God can change people the way He changed me.

Why are you so afraid to speak to me? I don't understand how you can work with me and talk and

laugh. And now? It's so sad that you can't even call me. I love you. I'm not going to freak out.

Matt, I say this with love and respect. You sound very unsure. The fact that I sent that video made it worse. You are still going through something. And so am I. We cannot throw fourteen years away. I'm about to publish a book. I have a meeting next week. Let's not worry about this. We need to take some more time.

October 20 was a normal day. I didn't tell anyone in my family what Matt had emailed me. I didn't want anyone to know because it was disrespectful, also I didn't want to give any life to it.

I was still saying my prayers three times a day. I was speaking God's promises over my life, Matt, our marriage, and our family. This situation had deeply affected my daughters. I felt sad for them. I knew they missed Matt too. Everything was out of place. I prayed for our family restoration, even though some days I wanted to give up and give Matt the divorce he said he wanted.

Then I remembered that I had been fighting all along for this marriage. God wants me to fight. He is the God of Restoration, not the God of divorce. I will not give up. We tend to give in too easily these days about marriage and divorce. I hope people will realize the other way and try to save a marriage. We take holy vows, then throw up our hands and say, "It didn't work out." We move on. I know there are situations that can't be helped, but I believe in the sanctity of marriage. That is why I'm fighting so hard for this.

I truly believe that God put Matthew in my life for a reason. We balance each other out. We push each other to make each other better. I once thought the love we shared was transcendent and would endure forever.

Chapter 24

On October 22, I awoke excited to have a phone call with my publisher, Jennifer. We met back in September at the Hershey RV Show. She was actually a fan of our show, and she walked over to our tent to meet us. She introduced herself to Matt, then she walked over to me and asked, "Hi! Do you want to write a book?"

It was so funny. I thought she was joking. That was the first thing she asked me. It was destiny. Jennifer was a little shy, but so delightful. She reminded me of a bright light. We briefly talked about me writing a book on RVing and our YouTube channel. We exchanged information and decided to have a meeting in a few weeks. I couldn't wait to talk to her again.

The phone call was scheduled for 4:00 pm. I wasn't really feeling the topic for my book to be about RVing. We got on our call and had small talk. She told me she had been so nervous about meeting me. I tell everyone I'm literally the same person on and off camera. Then something happened: I had an overwhelming sensation to talk to her, and I spilled all the beans about what was going on in my marriage. To me, talking with Jennifer felt familiar—as if I had known her for years. I had a strong intuition that it was safe to trust her. Instantly, she became my friend.

Telling people my problems was not my thing. Even my parents didn't know what was going on with Matt. I did not want to stress out or upset them. This was comforting for me. Jennifer listened to the whole story of how Matt and I had been apart, how he wouldn't talk to me, that we still work together, and no one knew what was going on between us.

Then I described my idea to create a faith-based book. I also told her about how God recently took my heartbreak away and replaced it with a peace too powerful to explain.

Jennifer and I brainstormed what I would write about. My book began to take shape. I was passionate about saving my marriage and my testimony, and my purpose was to encourage, inspire, and support other people who are going through similar seasons and hardships in their lives. I can relate, and I understand the indescribable pain that many endure. I wanted my readers to know how I managed each day.

I shared that there was only one way for me: The way the truth and the life. (John 14:6) If I did not have Jesus, I wouldn't get out of bed. I got emotional on the phone, finding it difficult to tell my story from the beginning.

Jennifer was so understanding and empathetic. She really was a light on my path. We talked about so much. She was getting goosebumps and so was I, which we both believed was a sign that we were on the right path.

I knew that the only way I was going to write this book was with God's blessing.

After our long call, Jennifer and I scheduled a Zoom meeting for two weeks later. At our next meeting, we planned to brainstorm on how to write my story. I could not wait to get started on this book.

After the book meeting, I felt a bit down after talking about Matt. Then, completely out of the blue, my ex-husband's wife messaged me, asking to talk by phone for a minute. That was strange because she had *never* reached out before. In fact, I had only met her a handful of times. She had always been very sweet and thoughtful, so I texted back that yes, we can talk.

When I called her, she asked, "Are you okay?"

"Yes," I responded. "I am good. What's up?"

"You were on my heart all of a sudden. I felt the need to reach out. Can I pray for you?"

Hearing that gave me chills. "Yes, thank you, I need it ."

We talked for a few minutes, and she prayed aloud for me, Matt, and the restoration of our marriage.

"Thank you for checking on me," I said.

After we said goodbye, I reflected on her thoughtfulness. It got me thinking about what was happening: Things just kept getting more bizarre for me. God is good all the time. He has been moving in my life like this. God knows when I need prayers and encouragement. My heart was overfilled with so much love. There were a lot of people praying for Matthew and me. I know there is power in prayer and in the name of Jesus.

I went into my bedroom and sat on my bed. I thought about the email again, realizing Matt never responded to my emails. What could I expect? I felt devasted. I couldn't believe this. I was in total shock and wondered, *Who is this guy? My husband would never do that to me. How can anyone do this to someone they love or used to love? Where is the respect? Didn't fourteen years of us being together warrant a face-to-face conversation?*

Just when I felt like God was slowly putting the pieces of my heart back together, it fractured again. What was God teaching me in this season? Must we be broken to be transformed?

Defeated and desperate, I got on my knees, shedding tears and hyperventilating. Memories from our marriage rapidly passed through my mind—our first kiss, Matt telling me he loved me for the first time, family times,

RV trips, milestones, promises, vulnerability to each other, and trust. *I really can't believe this. He is the love of my life, and I am his. It just doesn't make any sense.* I tried to take deep breaths so I could pray.

My Lord, My God. My everything,

I can no longer take this anymore. I can barely go on. My soul is in anguish. I can't take this heavy burden of sadness, heart-wrenching grief, the love I have for him, the loneliness, and the lack of communication. This is the most unimaginable pain I have ever suffered. Have mercy on me. Lord, I SURRENDER! I SURRENDER ALL TO YOU! I'm laying it all down at the foot of the cross. [Matthew 11:28] I said my life is yours. I give my life to Jesus. Praise your holy name. I know that you have a perfect plan for my life. I pray for your will to be done in my life. Not my will but your will. You said you would never leave me nor forsake me. [Hebrews 13:5] My Lord, hear my cries. I pray this in the precious name of Jesus. Amen.

I let it all go in complete surrender. Surrendering was extremely difficult. It's an uncomfortable feeling. No one wants to lose control over their life. We fear God will take things away when we do. We don't realize that God's plans for our lives are far more glorious than our plans. His plans are to prosper us, not to harm us, to give us a future and hope. (Jeremiah 29:11)

I didn't look at it that way—until Matt's email pushed me over the edge. I thought, *Surrendering is better than anything else at this point. I don't need to hold on anymore.*

I had tried to surrender before. But I hadn't really done it. But this time was different. I was at a desperate place in my life. I arrived at the end of myself. I had nothing to lose. I realized that I really have no control over my life anyway. We must remember God is in control of everything.

When I surrendered, I felt a significant shift in my spirit. I understood that God wants us to cast our cares and burdens onto Him. We are not meant to handle these struggles by ourselves. They are too much for us in our human bodies. (Matthew 11:28-30)

After all of this went down that evening, I felt a staggering feeling of exhaustion. I realized it was late, so I decided to go to bed.

I searched my bible app for a devo on hope. There were many to choose from. I knew that reading one would motivate me. Hearing the testimonies of other people gives you hope. The devo I chose talked about how not to lose faith in God, no matter the circumstances. Even if you can't see the outcome or see anything changing, trust in God. Then it referenced Joseph in the bible—How Joseph was sold as a slave by his jealous brothers, sent to Egypt, wrongfully thrown into prison, yet still kept his faith in God. Joseph's perseverance was preparing him for the most important job, the biggest blessing, and his purpose in life. Even though Joseph couldn't see that, he still believed in and trusted God's plan for his life.

The next day, my daily verse read:

Rejoice in our confident hope. Be patient in trouble, and keep on praying.—Romans 12:12 (NLT)

God profoundly spoke to me. By this time, I was convinced that every message I received pertained to my situation. Praise God, for He has not left me alone in my wilderness.

October 24 started out like normal. I woke up and said, "Thank you, Lord, for this day and my life." I went to get my morning coffee at Starbucks.

When I got home, I went to my bedroom to say my prayers. After my prayers. I felt a little lighter and different. I can't quite describe it. Maybe joyful and blissful? That was new!

I listened to Joel Osteen, who began to talk about Joseph and his brothers. I said aloud, "Why do I keep hearing about Joseph so much?"

Then instantly it hit me! *Enlightenment.* God started speaking directly to my heart, sending me the clarity I had needed all these months. Suddenly, I got it. It was like a puzzle being put together in front of me. The pieces were all falling into place. Suddenly, everything began making sense.

I felt confident assurance that God was speaking to me. I felt overwhelming joy, peace, and tranquility coursing through my body. I almost felt like I was on a cloud.

This was the joy of the Lord.

Chapter 25

It all became so evidently clear now. Everything that happened now fit into place. This divine revelation happened so quickly that I had to write everything down that I was seeing. A lot was being shown to me at once. It was like looking at an illuminated path.

I stood in my bedroom, crying tears of joy! I knew my purpose in life. I understood why this was happening to me. And most of all, I realized how much God loves me and cares about me. I have never had a divine encounter like that. I was astonished!

I will explain what God revealed to me.

The first thing that I was shown was Joseph's story in the bible. His brothers betrayed him, but they really had no choice because the enemy made them do it. God allowed it because He needed Joseph to get to Egypt.

Along the same lines, I understood that Matt's leaving was a process I had to go through of breaking and transforming, so that I could have an amazing testimony. I *had* to be broken so God could transform me for my calling.

The purpose of my story is to show that God is in control of everything. He needed me to share what I went through so that other people will know that there is a way. Even when you are broken, you are not alone. Turn to God. If you want to save your marriage, your finances, your business, your family, your health, your life. Don't turn to another person, turn to God. God does not want us to depend on any other person too much.

We are supposed to depend on Him. We have a jealous God. (Exodus 20:5) Put God first—in everything. If you want to be blessed, you must make God a priority in all things—your time, marriage, business, finances, and family.

I have always believed that I was meant to do something big in my life, and I am convinced that God called me to write this book to help more people. He even put two people—two Divine Connections—on my path at exactly the right time to bring this book to life. When I met my esthetician in June 2024, she told me to keep a journal of what God spoke to me. I hadn't kept journals before, but because she suggested it, I began to journal. Then, in September 2024, I met my publisher, who helped me transform my journals into the book you are holding in your hands.

My divine purpose was to write this book about my testimony, my story, to show how much God has changed me through this process. I've become a much better version of myself. God spoke to me this whole season.

While all of this was being revealed to me, I knew that I was going to get my husband back—just like Joseph got his family back. God knows what he is doing. He doesn't make mistakes. His ways are higher than our ways. (Isaiah 55:8-9)

My testimony is to show people that we can only get through life's valleys and storms with God. God provides love, strength, healing, and comfort.

You *could* do it without God, but it would be much more difficult. And then you will never know what God intended for you. God's plans are always perfect for us. But we often don't know God's plans because we don't listen to Him.

I have learned that life's storms always provide a lesson. We always endure them for a reason. The storm might have happened to teach you to trust or to stretch your faith.

I've also learned that despite the storm, you must hold on till the end. When the storm passes, you will receive blessings for what you have prayed for. The longer the hardship, the bigger the blessing. (James 1:12) (1 Peter 4:12-13)

I believe God has changed all of my pain into purpose. *This* peaceful, patient person is who I'm supposed to be in Jesus Christ.

Now I can't speak for what Matt has been going through. But I believe that all of this was to strengthen and improve our marriage—to make us come back together. To save us.

The reality is our marriage could never go back to the way it was. We were not in a good place. If it had kept going like that, who knows what would have happened. God's timing is perfect. He laid down a new foundation for us. *God* is the firm foundation and the rock on which our marriage will stand on.

From October 19 through November 9, I did not text or call my husband. However, I did faithfully read my daily verses, believing more than ever that God was speaking directly to me through these words.

October 26:

I pray that from His glorious, unlimited resources He will empower you with inner strength through His Spirit.–Ephesians 3:16 (NLT)

October 27:

And I am certain that God, who began the good work within you, will continue His work until it is finally finished on the day when Jesus Christ returns.–Philippians 1:6 (NLT)

October 29:

Obviously, I'm not trying to win the approval of people, but of God. If pleasing people were my goal, I would not be Christ's servant.– Galatians 1:10 (NLT)

November 3 my Strength for Each Day devo wrote:

God is also working in your life, even when you don't see anything happening, and He is present with you even when you don't feel He is near. Don't determine what God is or is not doing based on how you feel and what you see; make your determinations based on His word and His promises to you. Keep believing, and be assured that He is working. He will unveil what He has been doing, and you will be pleasantly surprised and overjoyed. Expect something good to happen.

Reading that encouraged me. I had not seen or heard from Matt since September 24. I missed him so much. We were supposed to be filming soon because the last videos we filmed were in Indiana. I continued to speak life and love over my marriage and family. I continued believing. Every day, I asked God for strength. I could not get through this without Him.

I continued with my prayers three times a day and Zumba four days a week. Here and there I visited with my friends.

November 6 daily verse:

I am leaving you with a gift—peace of mind and heart. And the peace I give is a gift the world cannot give. So don't be troubled or afraid.—John 14:27 (NLT)

I was amazed at how God spoke to me. It felt like these verses were meant for me. I was so thankful that I still had the peace that transcends all understanding. Nothing stressed me anymore these days.

On November 11, I texted Matt:

Hi Matt. Listen, we need to record. I still love my job. And I miss it. I am no longer sad or crying anymore. Let's get back to work. Nothing needs to be figured out right now. And I will not talk about our marriage or what you emailed me. All is well. Don't be afraid to come to the house. No one is mad at you. Okay?

No response.

I prayed and believed God would restore us so much that I continued thanking Him in advance for the restoration of our marriage and family, and for putting me back in my husband's heart.

That day, after my morning prayers, I got on YouTube, and a devo popped up. I decided to watch it.

This is what it said:

Even though they're gone, a deep peace settles in your heart. God's peace is a hint that separation is temporary and part of his greater plan.

If anyone doubts God's existence, I say, "Look at what is happening in my life. Way too much has happened to be a coincidence. Nothing happens by accident."

On November 15, I texted Matt:

Yoona is overdue for a vet appointment. She needs her heartworm meds and flea meds. Please make an appointment for her.

At that time, I didn't know where Matt was. I knew we had to film soon because we were running out of videos.

Two hours later, Matt texted me back:

Got her appointment scheduled. Can you film tomorrow or Sunday?

I texted:

Hi Matt! Sorry no, I'm having a surprise birthday party for Kayla. She is down here for her dad's wedding.

Matt:

See you Saturday.

Me:

Where am I going lol?

Matt:

It's up to you.

Me:

Tampa.

Matt:

Ok, I'm leaving Monday for San Antonio, we can do Ocala the following Monday.

Me:

Sounds good.

Wow. That hurt. That was the first time we talked since I left Indiana. I would see Matt for one day of filming, then he's leaving again. My heart skipped a beat. I keep thinking that any day it will hit him. He will finally wake up. I prayed for strength. I must stay faithful and believe. We can't let doubt take over. The enemy loves to sow doubt and fear. I know God is moving, even if I can't see it.

On November 16, my daily verse reminded me:

Do not be afraid or discouraged, for the LORD will personally go ahead of you. He will be with you; he will neither fail you nor abandon you.—Deuteronomy 31:8

I invited Matt to come to Kayla's surprise twenty-seventh birthday party.

He texted:

Hey, I won't be able to today. I'm really far behind on videos. Also, I just realized I need you to come to Ocala Sunday.

I texted:

Okay. I will be there at 10:30 am. If you need me earlier let me know.

Matt texted:

Sounds good.

I really needed to read my daily verse on the morning of November 17:

You are my refuge and my shield; your word is my source of hope.—Psalms 119:114 (NLT)

I was going to see Matt that day—for the first time in almost two months. Staying calm was going to take a lot of self-control. *Praise God that I have peace,* I reminded myself. I felt very calm and excited to see Matt. I felt like a teenage girl. I chose a cute outfit for filming.

I left my home to drive the hour to Tampa. On the way, I stopped at Wawa to grab a few things for Matt.

When I pulled into the dealership's parking lot, I texted Matt that I was here. He texted me which RV to go in. As I was walking over to the RV, I saw Matt walking toward me. I looked at him, smiled, and said, "It's really good to see you."

"It's good to see you too," Matt said.

My stomach flipped. "How are you?"

"You know, busy, busy, busy."

I wanted to hug Matt so badly, but we were at work so I held back. We had such a good time filming, laughing, and egging each other on. It felt like he was flirting with me. I felt our chemistry, raw and real, *How do we still have a great time filming?* I wondered. That was a mystery I hoped to crack soon.

After we were done filming, Matt said, "I'll be back in a week to film next weekend."

Before I got into my Tesla, I asked, "Did you read my messages?

"Yes."

"Are you good with us taking more time? Not proceeding with the D word?"

"Yes."

I breathed a sigh of relief. "Goodbye. I'll see you soon."

On my way home, I didn't cry, which was a first. I could still feel God healing my brokenness. I felt full of hope and faith. I made sure to thank God for this day with my husband. I was grateful to see him.

The next day's daily verse spoke to me:

God blesses those who work for peace, for they will be called the children of God.–Matthew 5:9 (NLT)

That day, I started writing this book. Writing the first part about how Matt and I met and fell in love was fun—easy. But as I got to the point of my heartbreak, writing made the pain fresh. I got so emotional, reliving the not-so-distant past. Writing—and rereading—my testimony was remarkable. The more I wrote and read about my experiences, the more I realized that many other people are going through pain too.

That thought made me sorrowful, though. I don't want anyone else to go through this. I pray and hope they will read my book and that it will speak to them and make them feel less alone. We go through storms in life. When we hear someone else's testimony, it encourages us. Look how God moved in my life! He will move in yours too!

These past months, I've read about the different phases of transformation. Honestly, before this all happened to me, I never even understood what transformation was.

Do not conform to the pattern of this world but be transformed by the renewing of your mind. Then you will be able to test and approve what God's will is—His good, pleasing and perfect will. (Romans 12:2)

And we all, who with unveiled faces contemplate the Lord's glory, are being transformed into His image with ever-increasing glory, which comes from the Lord, who is the Spirit. (2 Corinthians 3:18)

Transformation changes us. We come out of transformation totally different. I researched and created these six phases of transformation:

Phase 1: The Beginning: God starts by giving you a dream. It could be about your spouse, family, career, goal, or about what you could become. It could be a vision or a dream He puts in your heart. This could happen right before the storm starts.

Phase 2: The Decision: You have to decide to go after your dream. Dreams are worthless unless you do something about them.

Phase 3: The Isolation: In this time, God is purifying and refining you. He is more interested in your character than your dream. He wants you to learn to trust and depend on Him. While all this is happening, you might be alone and feel that no one notices what is happening to you. You will feel a yearning to be in God's presence more. Praying and reading the Word will not feel forced because you will *want* to spend more time in prayer and the Word. God is drawing you closer to Him. You find yourself slowly changing. You will become more patient and have more gratitude. You will feel more compassionate and want to help others. Your faith will get stronger all the time. Then you will develop trust in God, that he's got you, that His plan for your life is perfect. You will no longer long for worldly things. This is how we mature spiritually—how we grow and change. Let perseverance finish its work so that you may be mature and complete, not lacking anything. (James 1:4)

Phase 4: The Waiting: Here you are waiting for your breakthrough. Waiting is tough. This is where we must learn to be patient. But being patient is tough too. God's timing is perfect. The breakthrough will arrive exactly when it's supposed to. God never wastes our pain or our waiting. He will use our pain for a purpose. At this time, you might be learning how to persevere through your trial. God might be opening new doors for you that you never thought possible. He could also send different people into your life to encourage and help you with your dream. God wants to see us keep our faith, believing the whole time that he will be faithful.

Consider it pure joy, my brothers and sisters, whenever you face many trials of many kinds, because you know that the testing of your faith produces perseverance. (James 1:2)

Phase 5: The Desperation: This is when all seems lost. A relationship might end, or a business opportunity might fall through. You feel like you're at a dead end. Don't quit. The enemy wants you to quit. Be strong and faithful. Believe that God will come through—even if it looks impossible. That means you're almost at the end of your season. God likes to show His glory when it looks like there is no way from here to there. That's when you will undeniably know that it is God's hand.

Phase 6: The Deliverance: At this phase, God turns a crucifixion into a resurrection. He brings new life. He can raise a dead marriage. He can breathe life into a failed career or dream. He can bless you with a new business. He can give a child to infertile parents. Remember that there is nothing impossible for God. (Luke 1:37)

My November 19 Strength of Each Day daily devo reflected what I was learning about transformation:

Believing God:

Has a certain situation become so bad that you wonder if God can do anything about it? I encourage you to keep believing. Even if God doesn't fix your current circumstances, He can bring something good out of them. God wants us to believe, and He will work on our behalf. Keep believing no matter how long you have to wait and don't be moved only by what you see.

We need to have faith and believe in him. God is faithful. His promises are backed by all the honor of His name. (Psalms 138:2)

Faith is heaven's currency. And without faith, it is impossible to please Him. (Hebrews 11:6)

155

Chapter 26

The next day, I texted Matt:

Hi! I was checking to see if you still wanted to film this weekend. Tomorrow I'm busy all day. Saturday and Sunday should be fine. I would prefer Tampa. Whatever works better for you. Hope you have a great night! I miss my puppy so much.

Matt texted:

Looking to film Monday morning. I'm still in Texas.

I responded:

Ok no worries. Let me know Sunday night.

Matt:

Ok.

That was that. Well, I thought, *It's a good thing I texted him. I might have wasted a whole weekend waiting to get called to film.* He never tells me until the last minute or the day before. Even though I felt so much more at peace, and the heartbreak pain was gone, I was still going through the rollercoaster of missing him.

Sometimes at night, I couldn't stand the silence and darkness. I would get up, turn up the TV, and turn on all the lights.

In the morning before I was fully awake, sometimes I still looked for Matt. Fortunately, that didn't happen as often as it did for the first four months he was gone, but it still happened though.

I crossed my fingers that I would be going to my mother-in-law's house for Thanksgiving. I hoped Matt would put everything behind us for the sake of the holidays. I kept thinking he would ask me to go. *I guess we will have to see,* I thought.

November 22, my daily devo said:

Bold, faith-filled prayers and a positive attitude can change the course of your life and give you a future that is better than your past and your present. In response to your prayers, God may lead you to make some changes in the way you think, speak, act, work, or relate to others.

Well, I think I have been doing that for a while now!

On November 27, my daily verse said:

Most important of all, continue to show deep love for each other, for love covers a multitude of sins.—1 Peter 4:8 (NLT)

That day I was scheduled to record with Matt before Thanksgiving. I had asked him about his holiday plans, and he told me he was going to his mom's.

We had a good day filming, but as usual once the camera was off, Matt became a different person. As we were taking a break, Matt asked, "How many times a week do you work out? Do you work out with a partner? What do you do at the gym?"

Woah! I didn't expect that. I answered, "I go to the gym three or four days a week. I lift weights for about twenty-five minutes before my Zumba class. I don't have anyone. I work out by myself. I'm very active, and I almost run a 5k every class."

Matt didn't reply. I wondered what he was thinking.

After we finished filming and it was time for me to go, Matt drove me in a golf cart back to my car.

"Happy Thanksgiving," I said. "I will miss everyone."

"I'll miss you guys too." Matt replied.

I tried to hold back my emotions. I was ticked off because I didn't want to cry, but my tears have a mind of their own. They slowly ran down my face. "Can I have a hug? I love you."

Matt did not reply, but he gave me a hug. I noticed he got a little bit choked up.

"I got to go. I have a lot of work to do," he said.

I got in my car and said, "We need to batch record videos before the Tampa RV Show in January."

"I know. We will do that soon."

That was that. I got in my car to drive home. I cried so hard during the entire twenty-eight minute drive that I felt sick to my stomach. It felt unreal—our first holiday apart after thirteen years of Thanksgivings with Matthew, my girls, and my in-laws. I felt sorry for my daughters. This was affecting the whole family. I loved all of Matt's family. They were my family too.

I texted Matt:

Hi! I just wanted to say I'm sorry for earlier. I'm a little emotional because of the holidays. Try to enjoy Thanksgiving. You are overworked.

No response.

I really needed the devo God sent me on Thanksgiving:

Stand firm. The trial you are facing will come to end, and God will work good out of what you have gone through. You have to trust Him to do so. God is our strength through everything. Don't try to struggle by yourself. Ask God to help you with your troubles and hardships. He loves us and wants to hear our prayers and requests. Stand firm in your faith and don't quit or get weak in mind. Think good thoughts based on scriptures and God's promises. Be thankful for all He has done and is doing and what He will do in your life. Gratitude increases our joy and moves the hand of God.

Praise God! He is always finding a way to let me know, "I'm here! I haven't forgotten you!" More and more, I was convinced that nothing happens by accident.

Buoyed by that devo, I texted Matt:

Happy Thanksgiving! Hope you have a blessed day. All is well.

No response.

Overall, I felt great that day, especially considering it was my first Thanksgiving alone. My girls went over to their dad's house, then to a boyfriend's house. I reminded myself that they have their own lives too.

Truly, I didn't mind being alone that day. It gave me quiet time to concentrate on writing my book. I had no distractions, no one to feel sorry for me and ask, "Are you okay?"

My daughters must have asked me five times if I would go with them. It was very sweet of them to be concerned. But I needed to focus on my writing. Because I had written up to a point in the book where I felt the breaking all over again, I figured it would be best for me to be alone for that. I wrote for about five hours straight, and when I looked at the clock, it was 1:00 am. I decided it was time for bed. But first, I needed to say my nightly prayers.

Heavenly Father,

Thank you for this day and my life. I thank you for the miracles you do every day that I don't see. Thank you, Jesus, for your sacrifice for me so I could be forgiven for my sins and be reconciled to the Holy Father.

Lord, I'm grateful that you transformed my mind. Thank you for having humbled me and opened my eyes. You are the potter, and I am the clay. All the glory to you for the work you have done in me. I know you won't leave me here like this. I know you are still writing my story.

I pray to be more like you, that I would love like you, think like you, and speak like you. I pray that all the words that come out of my mouth will speak life and love. I declare life and love over all my family. I declare life and love back into my marriage and over my husband, Matthew's, life. I pray you will use me to be a vessel for your kingdom, for your glory.

Lord, I thank you for everything you have blessed me with. You have provided everything, and I know I would have nothing without you. Thank you for my husband and my children, family, and friends. Thank you for all the prayer warriors in my life—the divine connections.

Thank you for the YouTube channel, our subscribers, the Liquified business, our employees, and the warehouse. Everything good comes from you.

I know Matthew and I would have nothing if it weren't for you. You are in control of everything. I see your blessings all around us. I know your hand has been on Matt and me since the beginning. I know your hand is on our marriage and our businesses. Thank you. I pray that these businesses will glorify you. I'm grateful to have a job.

Thank you for the purpose you have given me. I'm honored and excited to do it. I ask for forgiveness for my sins. Make me a better Christian, wife, and mother. I can do nothing without you. Praise the name above all names, for He is good all the time and His love endures forever. Thank you that your plans for me are for good and not for harm. Thank you that you will turn my tears into joy and make beauty from the ashes. You are the way, the truth, and the life. Thank you that you will restore the years the locusts have eaten. What the enemy meant for harm, I know you will turn around for good.

Thank you, God, that you are faithful and that your promises are backed by all the honor of your name. Thank you for the marriage restoration on the way. I speak victory over my marriage. I declare your promises over my life and Matthew's. I stand on your word. You are the God of restoration, and there is nothing impossible for you. Since they are no longer two but one, let no one split apart what God has joined together. Therefore, a man shall leave his father and mother and hold fast to his wife, and they shall become one flesh.

I pray for protection over my husband, my family, my prayer warriors, and the divine connections from the enemy in Jesus' name. Lord, I depend on you. You are the only one I trust. Thank you that you are the Same God yesterday, today, and forever. Thank you for all you have done and for what you still will do. I pray this in the matchless name of Jesus. Amen.

That is only a very small part of what I prayed three times a day. My prayers were so much longer, and it would take me a lot of pages to include all of them. But I wanted to show the difference between how I used to pray to how I pray now. My prayers became more confident and expectant. I started speaking scriptures over my family's lives. Those are God's promises to us. You can always find something in the bible to relate to whatever you are going through.

I have become more faithful in my prayers too. You must *believe* you're going to get what you pray for, and you need to thank God for it in advance. He wants us to show that we believe and trust Him.

My prayer life has evolved over the past year because God has been changing me so much. All this time, I have grown closer in my relationship with the Lord. I am still amazed every day by Him. What will He do today?

Thank goodness for my new peace and calm from God, because Matt and I had no communication from after Thanksgiving through December 12.

Chapter 27

My birthday, December 4, was just another day for me. I stayed in and wrote. I tried to ignore that it was my birthday, but I thought Matt would at least text me. I never heard from him. That was like a stab to my heart, but I let it go quickly and forgave him.

I texted Matt:

Hi! Hope you had a wonderful Thanksgiving. I want to see Yoona. I have not seen her since September. And the girls haven't seen her since June. No one will be here for Christmas except me. Please let me know when I can get her. Also, we need to film. The Tampa RV Show is around the corner. Hope you have a great night! Btw our videos have been really good!

No response.

On December 6, my devo said:

We know how much God loves us, and we have put our trust in His love. God is love, and all who live in love live in God, and God lives in them.–1 John 4:16 (NLT)

Matt texted:

Can you film tomorrow and Sunday? One day in Tampa and the other in Ocala?

I texted:

Yes. Tomorrow, it needs to be Tampa. Are we safe to say 10:00 am in Tampa? I have plans at 4:00 pm.

Matt:

Okay, great.

The next day, I woke up at 3:23 am, restless, so I got up and prayed. That had happened the last time I worked with Matt before Thanksgiving. After praying, I went back to sleep. When I woke up, I realized I had been dreaming that I was praying. Weird. Never had that before.

I decided to get up and get ready for work. Because I had prayed so early that morning, I decided to pray again on the way to work. I was at the point where if I didn't make enough time for prayer, I felt wonky for the day. Prayer has helped me tremendously. I would not be able to do anything without God. He gives me strength.

Matt texted me to come in around noon because he was running late from his meetings. I decided to run errands before I left for work. I made perfect timing arriving at the dealership. I got there and went to the first RV. I always put my bag and phone in the front seat of the RV we're filming. I glanced down to check the time, and my phone said exactly 1:11 pm. These 1:11's and 11:11's had been showing up a lot lately, seriously, almost every day for the past month. Seeing that gave me a surge of hope, and I smiled a little on the inside.

The first thing Matt said when he saw me was, "The eleventh."

"Huh?" I asked.

"I don't know why I said that to you," Matt said.

I smiled and laughed.

"What is it?" Matt asked.

"Let's get started," I said.

I can't make this stuff up. I truly believe that was a message from God saying, "I'm moving in your life. I have not forgotten about you. Stay faithful and don't give up."

After we were done filming, I went back to my car. I was leaving early to go to church. I said bye to Matt, knowing I would see him in Ocala the next day.

The next morning, as I was leaving my house for Ocala, I got a text from Matt asking me to bring him hair gel and a brush. I said for sure. Good thing I hadn't left the house yet. Then I got a little irritable, *Oh, now I'm his wife.* I quickly shifted my thinking to gratitude, *It's good he still has a lot of things here at the house.*

When I got to the dealership, I asked Matt, "Where is your brush and hair gel?"

"Oh, I left them in the RV. I just came back from pickleball."

Okay, that makes sense. After filming, Matt told me he had to go on a quick work trip and would be gone a few days. I think he was going to Elkhart. I couldn't get over how much he travels and works. It made me nervous and concerned about his mental well-being. He had so much on his plate.

I texted him:

Hey, I just wanted to tell you something. You might not have heard it enough. Matt, you are truly amazing, and you blow my mind. You have worked so hard to reach your goals. You always believed, and look where you are. A lot of time, sweat, energy and sacrifice you have invested. I'm beyond proud of you. God has poured out his blessings! Praise him! Please don't feel awkward. Anything you need me to do, just tell me. I don't want you to deal with the mundane things. I want to help take some of the burden. Have a safe flight. I will see you later.

On December 12, a devo appeared in my YouTube feed: "Watch How God Is Restoring Everything the Enemy Stole." I watched it, and it reassured me that my breakthrough was very close, that what I had been praying for would come in God's perfect timing. It said that when God is working in your life and moving that you will experience the peace that surpasses all understanding. I still had that peace. Praise God!

I needed that encouragement because I sometimes felt doubt creep in. I didn't get to talk to many people about what was happening, but listening to devos and reading the word gave me hope. When I kept my eye on Jesus and not the storm, I didn't get as sad.

That video said that another sign that your breakthrough is close is increased opposition from the enemy. The enemy was trying to make me give up and quit before my breakthrough arrived. I had been praying for protection and strength. Then the enemy comes to kill, steal, and destroy. We must put the armor of God on to protect ourselves. (Ephesians 6:10-18)

I texted Matt:

Hi! Hope all went well with your work trip. I just wanted to tell you, your sticker renewal is here. Also, when can I have Yoona? Hope your day is blessed.

No response.

A few days later, Matt texted me, asking me to film in Tampa the next day at noon. I told him yes I would be there. For the next four days, Matt and I filmed about a month's worth of videos. I love my job and filming with my husband. I was trying to be very patient with everything, but it was painful when we filmed like we were happily married, but once the camera was off, we went back to our separate lives.

On December 19, I texted Matt:

Hi! Good morning! Are we working today?

Matt texted:

No, tomorrow.

I texted:

No, I'm busy all day. I have a meeting then appointments in the afternoon. Sat or Sun? Are you bringing Yoona today?

Matt:

Sunday we will film.

Me:

After work on Sunday. Can you bring Yoona over? I don't have the heart to tell Alyssa that you're not coming again. She hasn't seen Yoona in 7 months. Have

a heart, Matt. It's Christmas. This I hard enough on our family. Almost 14 years of Christmases spent with you, the kids, and your family. Do this for me. You can make time for this. We won't keep you long. I know you're so busy. I would be so grateful if you could do this.

No response.

On December 22, my daily devo shared:

People with a perfect heart want to be all God wants them to be. They let cooperate with the holy spirit to do the work in their lives. They love God's word and want to be obedient to Him. They love Jesus with all their heart and soul, mind, and strength. When they sin, it makes them sad. God has begun a great work in us and promises to complete it. (Philippians 1:6) He changes us gradually as we continue to be in fellowship with Him. Celebrate your progress as God works in you. Don't get concerned if you have a long way to go still. We grow spiritually each day, even if we don't see the changes immediately. We must be patient in God's work in us and ourselves. This is not an overnight transformation. If you don't succeed at first, then you are normal. We must keep going and never give up. Keep pressing on toward the victory.

That was an interesting devo. I had been going through my own transformation the whole time. I could relate to all the changes that have happened to me over the past year. Sometimes we don't recognize it when we are going through the process. It's an unsettling feeling, like we are being stretched. I finally realized that when I compare where I am now to where I was when this all started, I'm so grateful to God for changing me.

Sunday morning, I texted Matt:

Hi, what is the plan?

He told me he would drop off Yoona in thirty minutes, then pick her up later after the hockey game. He dropped her off, and she was so excited to see Alyssa and Anya (her Great Pyrenees puppy). She was happy to see me too. I started to cry. I missed her so much. After all, she was my baby. We had a great day with both dogs. We took them for walks, and they played well together.

Matt was supposed to get Yoona around 9:00 pm. As I was waiting for him, Yoona fell asleep on my bed. Poor baby, she probably missed it so much.

Matt texted:

I'll be there in 15 min. Do me a favor. I don't want to come in. Just bring her out and my stuff please.

I texted:

I can't. It's cold out. You have packages that are heavy and mail. I'm not lugging all this outside.

Matt texted:

Just leave them outside the front door so I can pick them up. This stuff really stresses me out.

I texted:

I'm not even stressed. I need to talk to you about business matters.

Matt texted:

Can you please just bring it out, and we will talk tomorrow at the dealership.

So I brought all his stuff to him with Yoona. I walked up to his truck, got in the front seat, and said, "I don't understand why coming to your own house is stressful. Matt, I am not the same anxious person I used to be. I have changed so much. God has done so much in my life. In fact, you look like *you're* stressed."

"I *am* stressed," he said.

"I'm so sorry. The last thing I want to do is make you stressed out. I do love you, Matthew."

"I know. I will always love you."

"Goodnight."

Then Matt reminded me we were working in the morning. I got out of the truck and walked into the house. I felt like nothing was changing, and he looked like he was still going through some things. Because it was late, I got ready for bed. I knelt next to my bed to say my prayers.

December 23 was our last day filming for 2024. We only had to film a few videos, and we got them done early because Matt had a meeting at 11:00 am. When Matt drove me back to my car in a golf cart, I said, "I will miss everyone for Christmas. It's going to be so strange. No one will be home. The girls will be with their dad."

"Why don't you go to see your parents in Seattle?" he asked.

"I can't. They went to the Philippines for a few months. I'll be okay. I'll be writing anyway. Are you still good with us taking the time to figure things out?"

"I don't know," Matt said. "I really don't want you to be waiting for me. I don't want to give you false hope. It's already been almost eight months."

That was a punch in the gut.

"I feel it would be better for both of us to go the other way."

"Let's think about it some more," I said. "Merry Christmas." Then I hugged him, but I didn't like the way he hugged me—very robotic and cold. I asked myself, *Where did my husband go? Is he still in there?*

I got in my car, and of course, I lost it. I had been holding on for so long. I kept thinking it's just going to hit him like lightning. I cried all the way home. I knew the holidays were going to be hard for all of us.

The words on my Christmas Eve YouTube devo caught my attention:

Beloved, know that this season is about God's glory, being revealed in and through your life.

Those words jumped out at me because in July, in one of the daily devos my daughter Kayla sent to me, God had told me that His glory would be revealed to and through me. That gave me chills.

I texted Matt:

Merry Christmas. I really do miss you and the family. Hope everyone is good. I hope you use the gift I got you.

[I bought him a leg and foot compression massage.] I remember how your calves and feet hurt. Tell everyone hi and Merry Christmas, that I love and miss them.

That night, I wrote more of my book. The empty silence in the house was magnified by the absence of laughter and gift opening. I took a deep breath, and a sudden feeling of misery washed over me. I was all alone, so I just sat there and let it go. This was the only time I have ever been alone for Christmas. When I was growing up, I had my parents, and later as an adult I had my children. That realization was overwhelming and just plain sad. My loneliness was palpable. My heart was heavy with grief, like a heavy weight in my chest. I felt so isolated. Did I belong anywhere? I poured my feelings into this book.

I wrote for about five hours, until 4 am on Christmas Day. Then I got up, went to my bedroom, said my prayers, and fell asleep.

When I awoke a little later on Christmas Day, I had very little to do. I reached out to family, wishing everyone a Merry Christmas. I watched some online church services, reminding myself I *was* not alone. God is with me. I spent a lot of time praying and worshiping. I started to cry, then stopped myself and declared God is faithful, He is in control, and He will keep the promises He put in my heart. Then I started praising God. God's plans for me are for good and not for harm.

I thought, *I know 2025 is going to be the best year ever. I'm walking into a new season of prosperity, purpose, marriage restoration, family restoration, salvation, and healing. I know God did not bring me this far to leave me here. Praise the name above all names, for His love endures forever, and He is faithful.* That got my spirits up, and I was happy.

No text or response from Matt.

Chapter 28

The day after Christmas was our seventh-year wedding anniversary. This hit me hard. I couldn't think of anything else but Matt. I posted our wedding photo to Facebook with the comment: It took me forever to find you. I will love you for the rest of my life.

I texted Matt:

Good morning! Sorry I can't ignore this day. Happy Kwanzaa. Lol seriously you know how I feel.

No response.

I couldn't bring myself to say "happy anniversary" to him. I would have said "happy Columbus Day" if our anniversary had fallen on that.

My devo the next day was helpful:

Many believers feel called to do certain things to serve God or to help other people. They may be called to ministry as a profession, or they may also be called to honor God and help others in various other professions or in ways that do not involve a career. They try to do what they believe they should do, but find that the right opportunities never come along for them. Doors that need to open for them seem to stay shut. I believe one reason this happens to people is that they are able but not stable. In other words, they have the skills and gifts they need, but they do not have maturity, character, or emotional stability that will be required to do what they feel called to do.

In today's scripture, Paul urges the Corinthians to "stand firm" and to "let nothing move" them. This means they are to be strong and to remain committed to what they know is right and to refuse to allow difficulties or perplexities to make them doubt their calling or stray from what they need to do. If you are eager to serve God and others but feel you keep running into roadblocks, you should ask God to help you stand firm and to let nothing move you. He wants you to fulfill his call on your life and to enjoy doing it.

On December 29, I read a Strength for Each Day daily devo (from May 31) titled: "When Will My Breakthrough Come?

God gives us dreams and visions (hope) for our lives, but He hides the exact timing of their manifestation. This, He reserves for His wisdom. Why does God withhold the timing of our breakthrough from us? Waiting is definitely a test of our faith, and it helps develop patience in us. Moses waited forty years (Acts 7:30), Joseph waited 13 years (Genesis 12:1-21:5). God must do many things to prepare us for the good things He has already prepared for us, and we should trust his process. If you are waiting for something right now and the waiting is frustrating you, I strongly encourage you to enjoy your journey because God will not be rushed. Every day that passes brings you one day closer to seeing your dreams come true, so enjoy the wait and remember that we inherit God's promises through faith and patience. (Hebrews 6:12)

New Year's Eve 2024 was not a good day. I woke up around 4 am with the stomach flu. I was sicker than I have been in years. I was literally vomiting for two days straight. My body was getting rid of 2024. What a way to celebrate the end of a year! Goodbye, 2024!

I somehow mustered the strength to text Matt:

Happy New Year! Every new year, you are always the first person I say it to. This year is going to be amazing. I hope you're doing good. I love you. Matthew, please forgive me for all that I have done. It means a lot to me to have your forgiveness. Can you just start with that? It's not good to carry that around. You are better than me. I am not the same person anymore. I really wish I could tell you all the things that have happened to me. It would blow your mind. Maybe one day you will ask me about it. I have no bitterness or unforgiveness

toward you. Let's have a remarkable 2025! I know the Tampa RV Show will be fun.

No response.

I was asking for forgiveness for all the things I had done wrong in our marriage, for all my faults and mistakes. I regretted throwing that D around so much. Matt once told me that he never thought that could be an option till I started saying it. I could have been a better wife.

I know now that God has changed my heart and mind. He revealed to me what needed to be changed. I am not the same person I was when this started back in May 2024. I will never take my husband for granted ever again. I will love him every day like it's my last. I know God will bring us together again. It will happen in God's perfect timing. God is faithful, and He is the God of Restoration. He is still writing my love story.

My verse on the first day of 2025 read:

"But forget all that—it is nothing compared to what I am going to do. For I am about to do something new. See, I have already begun! Do you not see it? I will make a pathway through the wilderness. I will create rivers in the dry wasteland.—Isaiah 43:18-19 (NLT)

That bible verse couldn't have been anymore aligned with my life. What a way to start my new year! I was still sick with that stomach flu. I texted Matt, asking him if he wanted to film this week. No response. I was basically bedridden because I was so nauseous and dizzy from that flu that all I could do was sit and think.

Sometimes doubt crept in, and I thought, *I have been waiting for so long. How much longer can I do this?* Then God would send me a devo or video telling me to hold on a little bit longer. I needed to constantly encourage myself. I do know that my God does not lie or change his mind. (Numbers 23:19) The enemy wants us to give up before we reach our breakthrough and reap our harvest of blessings. Don't give up! Don't quit what you have been holding on to! Start praising, "God is my sovereign, He is faithful, He is in control, I am a child of God, God's plans for me are for good and not for harm. God will not leave me like this. He will finish the good work he started in me. (Philippians 1:6) Speak life over your situation. Speak Victory!"

When I focus on Jesus and not my marriage problems, I am joyful. Praising carries me through. It gives me strength. It can do the same for you!

On January 8, finally feeling more like myself, I texted Matt a video called "Signs God Is Talking to You." It was about some of the things I believed Matt was going through. I don't know if he watched it.

I texted:

Matt, please take time for me when you get back. I have some business questions I need to run by you. I don't want to step on your toes. Let me know when you can talk. Keep warm there in Elkhart. From now on, leave Yoona here. She misses her house, her yard, and brother and sister.

No response.

My January 9 devotion, "For Such a Time as This," read:

I doubt that Queen Esther, as a young orphan girl, had any idea that she would eventually become the wife of a king, and that God would use her to save an entire nation. She probably never dreamed she would one day be considered one of the strongest women in biblical history.

What was the source of Esther's strength? Her faith in God. When an evil man threatened to annihilate the Jewish people, Esther intervened, asking her husband, the king, to spare them. Approaching the king without an invitation was very brave of Esther, and it went against the custom of her day. Her risk came with a great reward, as the king received her warmly and granted her request.

We see from today's scripture that Esther understood that saving her people was part of the reason she had become the king's wife. When you find yourself in an unlikely or challenging situation, remember Esther and realize that being there may be part of God's plan for your life. The source of your strength, like Esthers, is in your faith in God.

Wow! That made me think of my purpose in writing this book—sharing my story about my faith and belief that God will restore everything. I love seeing how God speaks to me in different ways.

Another devo came across my YouTube feed after prayer. It was about my breakthrough being very near, that no one can stop what God has planned for me, and that I am stepping into a new era of blessings.

I had been texting Matt all week.

No response.

On January 11, I woke at 3 am, feeling a restless shift in me. Lately I had been feeling like my faith has been renewed. I had been fasting and praying.

January 13 was the day before Industry Day at the Tampa RV Show. Over the past three years, we have gone to Industry Day. But I had not heard from Matt about this year's event.

Finally, on January 14th, I heard from Matt for the first time since before Christmas.

Matt texted:

Hey, I need to get inventory from the house.

I texted:

Are you here?

Matt:

I will be in about 10 minutes.

Me:

Ok

By the time Matt pulled into the driveway, I already had the garage door open.

"Hi, how are you?" I asked.

"I've been busy," Matt said, putting boxes of Liquified into his truck bed.

I started helping him. After we got all the products in, I gave him all his packages and mail.

"Thank you," Matt said, then got into his truck. "It would be totally okay if you did not want to attend the Tampa RV Show. It could be emotional for you—especially when people say how cute we are and mention our chemistry. I don't want that to give you false hope."

"No way!" I said. "This is what I do. I love our subscribers. They came there to see us. Some of them travel a very long way. I'm going. Matt, this is *our* channel. We did this together, you and me. I will be professional." I was standing by the driver's side door. Matt looked stressed and exhausted, like he was in pain. "Matt, are you okay?"

"I can't do this anymore," he said.

"What? You mean us?"

"I just can't."

"You want the D word."

"I was thinking a lot over the holidays," Matt said.

By that time, tears were streaming down my face. But I wasn't frantic or upset because something told me it's not over between us. "We still love each other. Matt, my God is not done with us. We were put together for a reason. You are my soulmate, the love of my life. Watch what God will do. God is going to move in you. You will know it. God's hand has been on us since the beginning. Our marriage will be restored. The growth that we are going through will save our marriage. I am telling you, God is in control of everything. I am that confident in my God. Just watch."

"I don't think so," Matt said.

"Well, then wait till after show season, and we will talk," I said. "Goodnight. I will see you tomorrow at the show."

I went back into my house crying. I proceeded to my bedroom for prayer. I said to God:

You tell me that when it looks like the end, when there can be no way, you make a way. I trust you, Lord. I know that you are in control.

Thank you that you are faithful. I know what you have spoken into my heart. I believe. Lord, I praise your name, the name above all names. There is no one like you. I trust your perfect plan for my life.

While I am speaking to God, peace washes over me. I wasn't anxious, just hurt. I know God will show His glory. I must be patient. We have to remember to praise God in both the good and the bad. For some reason, I was hearing 3 times in my spirit. That he would do this 1 more time, God gives me little pieces of my puzzle. Never all at once.

Chapter 29

January 15 marked the first day of the Tampa RV Show, which I was determined to attend. My Strength for Each Day devotion spoke of the same faithfulness:

God Is Faithful.

We have an enemy who continually seeks to steal, kill, and destroy us (John 10:10), and his name is Satan. But God has promised to protect us from the enemy if we put our trust in Him. We can only overcome fear with faith, so I remind you today to put your faith in God, claiming today's scripture for yourself and believing that God will always strengthen you and protect you from Satan. God is faithful, and He always does what He promises to do. He cannot lie, and He cannot fail us. All He needs in order to work mightily in our lives is our faith. He wants us to believe Him and enter His rest while He fights our battles for us.

What battle are you fighting right now? Don't make the mistake of trying to fight it alone. God is with you, and He will help you by giving you the strength you need to stay strong while He works in your life and in your situation.

But the Lord is faithful, and He will strengthen you and protect you from the evil one.–2 Thessalonians 3:3 (NIV)

I was grateful for that message and encouragement. It's amazing how God finds ways to speak to us. Sometimes He is speaking to us, and we don't notice. I said my morning prayers, got ready for the show, and left the house.

Often the first day of an RV show is rather slow. Usually, they get more crowded at the end of the week.

As usual, Matt and I were also selling Liquified at our big orange Matt's RV Reviews tent, and our Liquified customer relations manager, Kim, was selling it inside the building.

Matt and I actually were having a good day, laughing and joking with customers. Not that long ago, at the September Hershey RV Show, I had terrible heartbreak pain. But at this show, I felt joyful, happy, alive.

From the outside, no one would have known anything was happening between us. I didn't feel any anxiety from Matt, which was good. For the past few months, I had been picking up on his stress from time to time.

My January 16 verse said:

I said, "Plant the good seeds of righteousness, and you will harvest a crop of love. Plow up the hard ground of your hearts, for now is the time to seek the LORD, that he may come and shower righteousness upon you."–Hosea 10:12 (NLT)

The next day, my Daily Strength devotion reminded me to enjoy the journey.

The thief comes only to steal and kill and destroy. I came that they may have and enjoy life, and have it in abundance (to the full, till it overflows).–John 10:10

Jesus came to earth so we could enjoy our lives, but it will never happen unless we realize that life is a journey that involves many different ingredients, including a lot of waiting. Most of us just want to get to our desired destination or reach our goal, but actually, the joy is in the journey. When we do reach our destination, the journey is over, and before long we want another challenge. Everything in the earthly realm operates according to the law of gradual growth. Most things grow so slowly that the natural eye cannot even see it happening. Think of a tree. It is growing all the time, but we cannot see it grow. God could have arranged for everything to happen very fast, but He didn't. I think this is because we can only appreciate what we have to wait for. The anticipation of the good things to come is part of what makes them exciting. I urge you today to make a decision to stop being in such a hurry and simply enjoy your journey.

Today was the third day of the RV show. It did get a little busier, and people were stopping by our tent left and right to say hi to Matt and me. I was happy to be selling Liquified. It makes me feel productive, and I wanted to help as much as I could. Matt was bouncing back and forth from the tent to the building to help. We were selling a lot of products. It was so exciting to hear from the customers that they love Liquified.

Matt and I were getting along great. He was treating me much better than he had at the Hershey RV show, where I felt like he was ignoring and avoiding me. At least now in Tampa, he was laughing and talking with me. I knew God was moving.

On January 18, my verse read: *Even there your hand will guide me, and your strength will support me.–Psalms 139:10 (NLT)*

I also read this Strength Daily devotion:

God Hears and Answers Our Prayers.

Ask and it will be given to you, seek and you will find; knock and the door will be opened for you. (Matthew 7:7) The devil wants us to believe that God neither hears nor answers our prayers, but this is not true. You may think He hears and answers other people but not you, because you have too many faults. However, God's word reminds us of Elijah, who sinned just as we do, calling him "a human being with a nature such as we have…and he prayed earnestly for it not to rain, and no rain fell on the earth for three years and six months" (James 5:17). God has especially designed prayer for people who need His help. But if we do not believe that He hears and answers us, and if we do not ask Him for what we need in faith, we will not have it (James 1:6-8). We are invited to pray on every occasion, with all kinds of prayers and requests (Philippians 4:6). You can never pray too often or ask God for too much. God delights in our dependence upon Him. When we pray, if we believe we will receive, we will have what God has planned for us (Mark 11:24). We may not get it immediately, because there is typically a waiting period between our asking and receiving. This is a time when our faith is being tested, but let me encourage you not to give up during those times, because your answer is on its way. Come boldly to the throne of God and receive the help you need anytime you need it (Hebrews 4:16).

Today was Saturday, day four of the Tampa RV show. I was hoping it would be busy because that makes everything run smoothly. I got to the show early, around 8:30. There were a few people walking around, and before I knew it, the crowds were coming through. Then I started hearing, "Hey, there's Matt! Hi Andrea! We came to buy the Liquified show special."

"Thanks so much," I'd answer. We were having a buy-one-get-one-free sale, and we did really well all week. I was told that we hit all our sales goals. That was amazing. Praise God! He blessed us with a wonderful subscriber base and another incredible business with Liquified. All of this truly humbles Matt and me. We know we must stay grounded. We would not be in this position if it weren't for everyone's support.

Then one of my favorite YouTube friends spotted me. After a greeting and a hug, she said, "I knew I had to go and see you. Something told me to talk to you." The last time I saw her was at the Hershey show. She came over and gave me a big hug; she squeezed so tight. Then she looked at me and asked, "Are you okay? You seem different. I feel like the Lord was nudging me to come over."

That made me tearful. God is good all the time. He always puts people on my path who I will need. Sometimes I think they need me too. Her little visit really cheered me up. I was doing pretty good at that show, laughing and smiling. It is validating to see people who genuinely care about you.

About an hour later, another couple stopped by to see me. They commented to me that Matt seemed very robotic.

"He's just stressed out," I said. They had known us for five years, and for them to say that gave me pause. It did seem like he was just a shell of himself. I also thought that he was so busy with everything that he was not really himself. After the show was over, I headed home.

Matt texted:

"Hey, I know we're struggling right now…But I can't have you crying at the booth and praying. This is why I said you shouldn't work the show. Tomorrow is game day. If you're unable to be 100% that's aok. Please just stay home. If not I'll see you in the morning.

I texted:

I wasn't crying. This thing with you kicking me out is not happening anymore! People come over to me and say, "Something told me to see you today." And hugged me so tight. That's why I got emotional. Not cause of you! Everything isn't about you. I know you think the world revolves around you. I'm sorry to tell you this, but it doesn't. One day you will experience God's presence, then you will understand. Stay in your lane!

The last day of the Tampa RV Show started with rain and the threat of thunderstorms. That didn't look good. I forgot Matt was leaving for Arizona that night. He lost his jacket, and I knew we had one at home.

I texted Matt:

Good morning! You will need a jacket for your trip. It says 30 degrees in Quartzsite at night. I will bring you a jacket from your closet just in case.

No response.

I texted:

I'm here at the tent. I have your jacket if you need it. Everything is blowing over from the rain and wind. There was some lighting too.

I texted:

Matt, Wil, and Kim were in the building, where it wasn't raining and blowing.

No response.

I texted:

I'm getting drenched. It's bad. Even with a poncho. Everything is falling over.

No response

I texted:

Thank God. General people are putting our tent down.

No response.

At that point, I figured I could either stay where our tent was being dismantled around me and get soaked, or I could run and find another tent that was still up. I found another tent, which was where I stayed for about an hour. The Weather Channel predicted it was going to rain all day, and there were hardly any people at the show. What a bummer! I decided I wasn't going to stay outside all day in the rain, so I left early. I didn't get to say goodbye to everyone. No worries. They know I love them.

When I got home, I changed out of my wet clothes. I was pretty down about the weather not cooperating for the show. It happens, I suppose. I went to my knees for my afternoon prayers. When I was done, I decided to grab some yogurt and catch up on writing my book. I wanted to tell Matt a couple of things, so I texted him at 5:30 pm:

Text me when you get back. Hope sales are great there! Have a safe flight! [prayer emoji.] I love you.

No response.

I texted him before midnight:

Yesterday is gone; tomorrow is not promised. I live for today. I love you, and I'm still in love with you. God has kept you in my heart for a reason. You just can't ignore and forget the life we have. And our journey. You look so lost, Matthew. I have known you for a very long time. Something is not right with you. You don't seem happy about anything. I pray you find yourself before

it's too late. You are in my daily prayers. I do love you so much. Even when you're being mean. I know that is not who you are. If you need me this week in Arizona, I'm here. I can leave anytime.

No response.

My daily verse for January 20 was:

Love each other with genuine affection, and take delight in honoring each other.—Romans 12:10 (NLT)

Thank you, God, for sending me messages.

The next day, I texted Matt:

Hey! I hope sales are going great. I did clear my schedule next week. I see we will run out of videos soon. So, I'm good with any day and time. Let's try to get a good back log of videos if we can.

No response.

I was beginning to feel very sad again, missing him so much. It was always tougher on me after I saw him. I kept getting doubts in my head. The enemy was feeding my thoughts like:

"You have been waiting for so long."

"It's not going to happen."

"Nothing is changing."

"You could be doing anything you want right now."

I knew the enemy wanted me to give up. I rebuked those thoughts right away. I say: No weapons formed against me shall prosper. (Isaiah 54:17) I had been fighting for my marriage all this time. I was not going to quit.

After those doubts stopped, I began experiencing calming peace—even though my current situation looked different than what I believed it would be at this point. After what Matt said to me about the D word, it looked like the end.

I refused to listen to that. I know my God is faithful, and His words do not come back void. I had been in the waiting season for so long. It had been 245 days since

Matt left. I continued praying and trying to hang on, finding strength through God's word.

A few friends of my friends I talked to encouraged and supported me. If you are going through a tough season or hardship, it is so important to surround yourself with like-minded people. Find friends who will speak life into you and give you strength.

Chapter 30

January 22, my Daily Strength devotion ironically asked, "Where Do We Find Strength?"

I love that God is ever-present. There is never a time when He is not with us, but we may miss out on the help He is ready to give us by forgetting about Him and trying to do things in our own strength. He wants us to lean and rely on him. Leaning on God for absolutely everything is not an indication of weakness; it's actually a sign of wisdom. Jesus says that apart from Him we can do nothing. (John 15:5) We may do things, but we will struggle and be frustrated because nothing works with ease unless we invite Jesus to be involved in it.

What are you trying to do on your own that is frustrating you? Whatever it is, stop. Then tell the Lord you are sorry for leaving Him out of it and ask Him to take the lead in your situation and give you the grace to follow Him.

I have tried many things on my own, such as changing myself, changing my husband, and changing my children. I saw their flaws and wanted to correct them, but only God can change a human heart. I also tried in my own strength to make my ministry grow, but that ended in misery too. I have learned to ask God for what I need and lean on Him to bring it to pass. Anytime I forget about this, before long I find myself struggling again trying to do it myself. Let go and let God show His strength through you. God is my refuge and strength, an ever-present help in trouble. (Psalm 46:1)

It was funny how that was the daily devotion after the day I had yesterday. These things keep happening to me. How could I not believe them? God answers me in so many ways. I sometimes ask myself, *Is this really happening, or is it a coincidence?* These answers and occurrences happen so frequently. It is like God knows I'm struggling, then He sends me messages or devotions to keep me going—although the devotions and verses on the bible app go by date, so they were obviously written in the past. Who could know what I would be facing? God, that's who!

On January 23, I went to Zumba class, then I went home and did some writing. When I was watching YouTube, a video popped up on my feed that almost made me cry. Its message resonated in my soul. It was titled "God Still Wants You Both Together." I shared the link with Matt, of course, and I got no response. I wondered if he ever watched it.

The video was about why you can't stop thinking about your spouse. Even when you try to distract yourself, they still come up in your mind. No matter how hard you try, you can't let go. God uses thoughts to keep us in each other's minds while He works.

That video helped me to see that God is preparing us for a reunion. The season of separation was necessary for our growth. He is preparing us for restoration. God speaks through peace. He is trying to align us with His will. We both had to go through healing, growth, and transformation. This way when we come back together, we will be better for each other. Restoration will be a blessing to us both. Wow! That was talking to me. That night, I prayed for more clarity. I asked God to help me hold on.

On January 24, when I opened my phone, there was a devo right at the top of the page saying, "3 Reasons You Should Wait."

1. Even when it seems impossible, a part of you holds onto hope. This hope isn't by chance, but it could be God encouraging you to wait in faith for His timing. Stay anchored in prayer and trust Him. (Hebrews 11:11)

2. Friends, family, or even strangers bring them up unexpectedly. This could be God's subtle way of showing you that their role in your life isn't finished yet. Pay attention to these moments. (Proverbs 15:22)

3. During the separation, you notice areas in your life that God is asking you to improve. He could be working on both of you individually to strengthen the relationship when it's time. Growth now leads to a better future. (James 1:4)

A few days later, I watched a devo on YouTube that shared three key reasons God removed them, but a reunion is meant to happen.

1. God removes people to protect you from unhealthy patterns that need to be addressed. He allows separation so that both of you can reflect on what needs to be changed. When the time is right, He reunites you under healthier and more stable circumstances. This separation teaches you valuable lessons about yourself and your role in the relationship. (Psalm 34:17-18)

2. Sometimes God removes someone so you can both focus on your individual purpose. This time apart can help you discover the calling God has placed on your life. By walking in obedience, you prepare yourself for the relationship He has planned for you. When you come back together, your shared purpose will strengthen your bond. (Timothy 1:9)

3. God may use the time apart to show you how much you value the relationship. Absence can make you realize the things you took for granted and inspire gratitude. This perspective helps you approach the relationship with more humility and appreciation when a reunion happens. The break becomes a blessing in disguise. (Romans 12:10)

After my gloomy day, I needed that. Praise God that He hears us. He is our refuge in times of trouble. Whenever you feel sad or hopeless, remember that God is our strength. (2 Corinthians 1:3-4) (Psalm 46-1)

I texted Matt:

Hi. Please let me know what's going on. I have things I need to figure out. Thank you.

No response.

I needed him to let me know a schedule for filming or something.

The next day, I texted Matt:

Hey, are you okay? Can you tell me if I'm working this week? Please communicate. We are still a team.

No response.

The next day, I texted Matt:

Hey, I don't know what I did. This is work, Matt. I know you're going through a lot and you're super busy. All I ask is for an answer. I don't care if you respond that you don't know. Just answer me back. That's all. This treatment is too much. I am sorry to bother you.

No response.

February 1, I read an inspiring verse:

Let us then approach God's throne of grace with confidence, so that we may receive mercy and find grace to help us in our time of need.–Hebrews 4:16 (NIV)

The past four days had been heavy on me. I had been crying again—not the out-of-control crying, but the sad, lonely tears. I was experiencing an overwhelming feeling of missing my husband. I was exhausted and weary. I woke up at 4 am that morning, so I decided to pray. I had spent almost a year battling for my marriage, and I was not going to quit.

That was an especially tough day for me because I had to put our cat Mochi down. Matt had rescued her when we lived in Maryland. We got her when she was about four years old, and now she was almost eleven. She had a fatal liver disease, and the vet told me she was suffering. I couldn't take that. So I had her put to sleep. I didn't know how or when to tell Matt. I waited till the show was over in Quartzsite and then texted him. I felt so bad, but I believed he had the right to know.

I texted Matt:

Good morning. I'm so sorry to tell you this way. I never know when I will see you. I had to put Mochi down. She had a fatal liver disease, and she wouldn't have made it much longer. I didn't want her to suffer. It's tough on all of us. We take comfort that she is in a better place. I thought maybe you would want to know.

Also, I can film tomorrow, Thursday, and Friday morning. Let me know the plan. I hope all went well in Quartzsite. You probably are exhausted and jet lagged. If you need me for anything, I'm here.

No response.

I knew that Matt was back in Florida because he had been posting videos with a few manufacturer reps and salespeople. That was fine. I was good with that. I just needed to know what's happening because if I wasn't needed for work, I could go visit my daughter or my parents.

I texted Matt:

Hey. I know your mind is all over the place. You're going through a lot. I can tell. I used to be the one you confided in. The only one you trusted. Matthew, I'm here if you need to talk or vent. I can handle anything. I promise you I'm a good listener. And I would never judge or lecture you. That's not who I am. I know what it feels like not to have that "one" person. The one who knows and understands you. I say this as the most honest, loyal, and faithful friend you have. 14 years is no small matter. I know you. No matter what is going on, you can always talk to me.

No response.

That night, after not getting a response to any messages, I was frustrated.

I texted Matt:

I don't know why you are acting like this. What did I do? I need to work. Stop ignoring me and just answer me.

Two hours later, Matt texted:

Hey, not ignoring you. We will film after I get back from Salt Lake City.

The Salt Lake City RV Show was from February 13 to 16. If he was already back in Florida, that doesn't make any sense to me. I had almost ten days to film.

I had been having a lot of dreams lately about Matt and me. Usually, I didn't remember the actual dream after I woke up—just the intense feeling of missing him. That afternoon, a devo came up on my phone about dreams. It said not only is it about my subconsciousness, but it could be that he is thinking about me a lot. Apparently, when you have a soul connection, you can feel what the other person is feeling. Time and distance don't matter.

I thought that was a little strange. Maybe that was why I was having chest pains here and there. I might be feeling Matt's anxiety and stress. I knew he had a lot going on with Liquified.

Back in November 2024, I talked with my doctor about the chest pains, and he told me it was delayed panic attacks. I told them I'm not stressed! They ran a whole bunch of tests and concluded that everything was fine with my heart.

I texted Matt:

Hey. Hope all is well. I know you hate me. I'm sorry, truly sorry, for whatever it is making you this way. It's so sad that I NEVER know what is going on. It hurts that I'm the last one to know anything. If you are uncomfortable talking to me and considering me part of this team, what can I do? I can never get away from you, like you will never get away from me. We are intertwined in each other's lives. This is what we built

together. And I still have a lot of fun doing this with you, despite how I'm alienated from everything. I hope you don't think ignoring me and a piece of paper will take our feelings away. And I think we have been getting along better in our videos. Try to consider that I am a part of this team. I deserve to know what's happening.

No response.

On February 5, Matt texted:

Hey. Can you leave all my mail in a bag on the front porch for Wil to swing by and pick it up? Ty.

I texted:

No, it will have to wait till I get home.

Matt texted:

Oh, OK. Yeah, later tonight.

Me:

Oh, btw do you need me for filming? It's weird that I have been off so long.

Matt:

Yes, I need you when I get back from Salt Lake City.

Me:

Thanks for letting me know

Matt:

Thank you. Let me know when you got all the mail and he will be on his way to swing by and get it.

Me:

Ok will do. Please take Yoona to the vet.

I texted about an hour later:

It's on the front porch,

Matt:

Thank you.

Then a few hours later, I saw on a YouTube video that Matt was selling our travel trailer. I was floored. I thought he would at least have told me, even though I knew that eventually selling it was our plan from the beginning when we bought it.

I texted Matt:

Wow! You're selling it. I know that was the plan from the beginning. I do hope and pray that you're not going to surprise me anymore. Make sure to take the tags off and get them to me if you sell it. Thank you.

The good thing was that I had so much time and energy to write my book that I was getting close to being finished. This break might have been divinely orchestrated.

I tried not to get discouraged by Matt's cold texts. I knew I had to keep pushing through. I had to hold on. After saying my prayers for the night, I got into my bed. I started scrolling through YouTube. Lucky me, a devo popped up two minutes later.

This is what it said:

1. Every time you try to let go, God sends undeniable confirmations to hold on. Whether through scripture, dreams, or unexpected messages, He keeps reminding you that this isn't over. (Isaiah 55:11)

2. Your heart is at peace even though the situation isn't perfect. God's peace is a major sign that He is still working, even when things feel uncertain. (John 14:27)

3. Letting go feels forced, as if you're moving ahead of God instead of waiting on Him. If it doesn't feel right, it may be because God is asking you to be patient. (Lamentations 3:26)

4. You see signs of personal and spiritual growth while holding on. If God is using this season to build your character and faith, He may be preparing you for something greater. (Romans 5:3-4)

I didn't know how that happened. It was speaking to me. It couldn't be a coincidence. Sometimes I thought I was going a little crazy. I believe everything happens for a reason. That devo was so relatable to my situation because I *have* gone through a lot of spiritual growth.

Valentine's Day dawned with trepidation in my heart. How would I feel? I watched a devotion on YouTube that shared:

God is saying to you today, you're about to receive a harvest of blessings. I am honoring the seeds you have sown, the prayers you have prayed, the worship you have offered, the sacrifices you have made, and the perseverance you have shown. Get ready. An outpouring of blessings are coming your way.

That same day, Walmart trucks were picking up cases of Liquified at our warehouse to sell in their stores. That was a divine blessing. I praised God. He is so amazing. He is in control of everything. God has blessed us so much. This was a very emotional moment for me. I knew how hard my husband worked for this and the sacrifices that were made.

I texted Matt:

I'm so proud of you!! I prayed for blessings over our businesses every day. God hears our prayers. It's exciting to see it going to Walmart. May God continue to bless you.

No response.

I texted Matt:

I'm sorry I'm not with you to say congratulations. I know personally what you have put into this. The sacrifice and time. It makes me cry because I have watched you all these years. Never taking no for an answer and never giving up. I'm just joyful and happy. I truly hope you are content and finally feel your accomplishments. I don't know anyone more generous and more deserving than you. This comes from the bottom of my heart. I will always love you.

No response.

Chapter 31

February 18 was Matt's thirty-fifth birthday. My daily devo was on "Living in the Now."

Today we have faith that God will take care of any mistakes we made yesterday and that He holds tomorrow in his hands. This alone allows us to enjoy and live fully today. Today is the gift we have from God. To miss the joy and opportunities it holds due to regret over the past or dread of the future is not God's will for us. True faith must always operate in the "now" season of our lives, and faith alone enables us to be at peace and enjoy the present moment. Everything is in God's hands, and He has a good plan for each of us. (Jeremiah 29:11) Rather than dreading or feeling apprehensive about the future, we can live with expectancy regarding it. Expect something good to happen to you and through you. As you do, you will find a joy that only God can give coursing through your soul. Let go of what lies behind (Isaiah 43:18-19; Philippians 3:13-14) because God is doing something amazing in you and in your life right now, and you don't want to miss it. Now faith is the assurance (the confirmation, the title deed) of the things (we) hope for, being the proof of things (we) do not see and the conviction of their reality. (Hebrews 11:1)

I texted Matt:

Happy birthday! I hope you have an amazing day!

No response.

I texted Matt at 3 pm:

Hey. We need to talk. I need to know what is going on.

No response.

I texted Matt:

I have seen so many videos on our channel where they are just not mentioning me. The comments are coming in. "Where is she?" I felt like after a few months, something needed to be said. Not talking about me is weird.

I texted Matt around 8 pm:

Matt, this is business. I am still part of the channel. I miss work. Please let me know what you're thinking. I know the show is this weekend. If you are thinking next week for filming, please let me know. I do hope you're having a great birthday. ☺

No response.

All day, I had been feeling emotional. I especially missed Matt on his birthday. I hadn't seen him since the Tampa RV Show about a month ago, and the communication has been little to none. I had been weepier the past few weeks. I was honestly tired of missing him. Even through all this, I was still in love with him. God has given me a loving, forgiving heart.

I think when you go through something that breaks you, it changes you. The little things that would normally have upset me don't shake me. All that matters is this one life and what we do here.

That night before bed, I went to say my nightly prayers. My prayer life was always evolving. Because I had been much busier, I changed from praying three times a day to longer prayers twice a day. I prayed:

Heavenly Father, Abba, My God, My Lord, My Savior, My everything, I come boldly to your throne of grace. I pray for your presence to surround me. Holy Spirit, you are welcome here. Please lead and guide me in my prayers. Thank you, Lord, for this day and my life. Thank you for protecting me, for all the mercies you give me for each breath I take. Thank you for all the miracles you do in my life. Thank you, Jesus, for your sacrifice. For your innocent, holy sacred blood that was shed for me so I could be forgiven for my sins and be reconciled to the Holy Father. I am eternally grateful to you. Thank you for loving me first and loving me unconditionally, I know you will never leave me nor forsake me. (Deuteronomy 31:6) I'm grateful for your love and light, mercy, grace, and your peace and joy that surpasses all understanding. (Philippians 4:7) I rejoice in you, Lord, always. I pray that you will restore the joy of your salvation in me. (Psalm 51:12) I want to be joyful in you every day of my life. You are everything to me, and I can do nothing without you. Lord, I depend on you, and I only trust you. You know my heart and soul better than I know myself, and you know I love you more than anyone. You are first in everything in my life.

Lord, thank you for transforming my mind. (Romans 12:2) You have changed me. You are the potter, and I am the clay. Thank you for making me into who I'm supposed to be, in Christ. I know that you will finish the good work you started. Lord, I know that you will not leave me here like this, that you are still writing my story and my testimony, which I pray will glorify you. I ask that you make me more like you, to love and think like you, for my words to always be encouraging, kind, positive, loving, uplifting words that speak truth, life, and love.

I declare life and love over my life, Matthew, and our marriage. I speak victory over our marriage and lives. I declare life and love over my children. I speak victory over Kayla, Joe, Alyssa, Bella, and Jayden. I would speak life and love into anyone who needs it. I pray you will use me to be a vessel for your kingdom, for your glory. Lead and guide me wherever I need to be. I seek your kingdom; I pray for your will to be done in my life.

Thank you, Lord, for all the blessings and provisions you have given me. Jehovah Jireh, you have provided everything I need. I know I would have nothing without you. Thank you for family, friends, all the prayer warriors, and divine connections. I'm grateful for my Zumba instructors and friends. Thank you for my health. Lord, I know you are in control of everything. Thank you for our YouTube channel, each and every one of our subscribers, our Liquified business, our employees, the warehouse, and now Walmart. I'm grateful to have a job. I pray that these businesses would glorify you. Look at what the Lord has done. It is marvelous in our eyes. (Psalm 118:12) I know Matthew and I would have none of this if it weren't for you. I know you have blessed us abundantly. You are good all the time, and your love endures forever.

Lord, I ask that you forgive me for my sins. Wash me clean in the blood of the lamb. I am human, and I fall short. Help me to be a better Christian, a better wife, and a better mother. Thank you for the purpose that you have given me. I am honored and grateful for it. I pray that you will lead and guide me in this, that it would glorify you and be a blessing to others.

Thank you for putting Jennifer in my life. I know you put her on my path. I pray for blessings over Jennifer and her family, guidance and protection. Thank you for my esthetician, another divine connection. I pray for blessings over her and her family, guidance and protection.

I cast all my cares and worries upon you, for I know you care for us. Your yoke is easy, and your burden is light. (Peter 5:7) You know what I need before I even ask. Lord, make me a better steward of my finances, the blessings, and the blessings to come.

Thank you, Lord, for fighting my battles for me. Thank you that no weapon formed against me shall prosper. (Isaiah 54:17) That I am the head and not the tail, I am more than a conqueror in Christ. Thank you that I am a child of the most high God. I am fearfully and wonderfully made. I am a masterpiece and one of a kind. (Psalm 139:14) Thank you that your plans for me are for good and not for harm, but to prosper me and to give me a future and a hope. (Jeremiah 29:11) I will be prosperous. I shall lend and not borrow.

Thank you, Lord, that you go before me and order my steps.(Psalm 37:23) That the number of my days are fulfilled and that the latter days will be better than my former days. That the best is yet to come. (Job 8:7) I believe that. Thank you, that my children will be mighty in the land, and as for me and my house we shall serve the Lord. (Psalm 112:2) Surely his goodness and mercies will follow me all the days of my life, and I shall dwell in the house of the Lord forever. (Psalm 23:6) Thank you that I will have life abundantly. I shall live and not die. By your stripes I am healed. (Isaiah 53:5) Thank you, that after I have suffered a little while that you will restore, support, and strengthen me and place me on a firm foundation. (Peter 5:10) You are the rock upon which I stand. Thank you, that you will turn my tears into joy and make beauty from the ashes. (Joel 2:25) I know that you work all things together for the good of those who love you, who are called according to your purpose. *(Romans 8:28)* Thank you that you are faithful and that your promises are backed by all the honor of your name. *(Psalm 138:2)* Lord, thank you that what the enemy has meant for harm, you will turn it all around for good and flip the script. *(Genesis 50:20)* I know that you are not a man, so you do not lie or change your mind. You have never failed, and you never will. *(Numbers 23:19)* I praise your name, the name above all names. You alone are worthy of all honor, all praise and all glory. Thank you that you hear my prayers. Before they call, I will answer. While they are still speaking, I will hear. *(Isaiah 65:24)*

Lord, I pray for protection over my husband, Matthew, our marriage, and our commitment to each other. My children, Kayla, Joe, Alyssa, Bella, and Jayden: The enemy has no place in our lives. I look to you, my sovereign Lord. You are victorious, the battle is won. I look to you for the power and authority that is in the name of Jesus. Protect my family and marriage from the enemy in the mighty name of Jesus, my Lord and Savior. Every knee will bow at the name of Jesus and confess, "Jesus is Lord." Thank you, Jesus.

I pray for restoration for our family. Lord, soften their hearts for forgiveness. Surround them with your love, presence, goodness, and light. I pray that you will invade my husband, Matthew's, heart and life. I pray someone will speak life into him. I know he will be saved.

Thank you, Lord, for saving our marriage. Thank you for rebuilding our marriage on you as our firm foundation. You are the rock upon which I stand. I can do nothing without you. I pray you will lead and guide us in all we do in our lives and marriage to follow you. Use us to do your work and to serve you. Thank you for the time that we have had apart. You have made our marriage stronger and greater. You have made us closer through you. We are one flesh connected through our vows and you. I declare your promises over our marriage. Since they are no longer two but one, let no one split apart what God has joined together. *(Matthew 19:6)* Therefore, a man shall leave his father and his mother and hold fast to his wife and they shall become one flesh. *(Genesis 2:24)* Let your wife be a fountain of blessing for you. Rejoice in the wife of your youth. *(Proverbs 5:18-20)* I declare your word over our marriage. You are the God of restoration. You told me to look *with faith-filled expectation, that you would reveal your glory in this situation. I pray that my husband will undeniably know that it's your hand moving in him and in our marriage. I know the promises you have spoken to my heart. I speak victory over our marriage.*

I pray that your will be done here on earth as it is in heaven. Lord, please lead and guide Kayla and Joe to follow you. I pray for your presence in their lives. Please keep them safe and give them good health.

I pray that you will heal Alyssa's MS. You are Jehovah Rapha. By your stripes we are healed. I believe you can heal her. I know you can. I pray you will reveal your glory in this and that your presence will be known in Alyssa's life.

I pray that you would invade Bella's life with your presence, love, light, and goodness. I pray for her salvation, I know she will be saved. I pray that you will give her purpose for her future, that she would know she is made for more. Only you know what her future holds.

I pray for all my prayer warriors. I'm so grateful for all of them. I don't know where I would be without their prayers. I'm so moved by all the prayers for Matthew and me. For when two or more are gathered in your name, you are there. There is power in prayer and power in the name of Jesus. I pray for prosperity, blessings, guidance, and protection from the enemy in Jesus' name. Thank you for each and every one of them.

I pray for all the ones in this world who don't know you. I pray they will get the chance before it's too late. Lord, give us the biggest revival the world has ever seen. I pray you will light hearts on fire, that it will light up this world. There are people lost, in pain, in the dark, and in chains. We need you, Lord. I lift my friends and families for healing. Comfort and heal them. You are closest to the brokenhearted.

I pray for the protection of Israel and the people from the enemy in Jesus' name. I pray you will lead and guide their government and leaders. I pray for protection for our nation, our president, his family, and his administration from the enemy in Jesus' name. Make your presence known in our government and president.

Thank you for your words. I am seeking you every day. I pray for wisdom, knowledge, understanding, and discernment in your word and in my life. Lead and guide me to always follow you. Use me to be a blessing on someone else for your glory.

I know that you are faithful and are working all things together for my good. I see you moving all around me. You are the light of the world. To God be all the glory. All heaven and earth are filled with your glory. You are the same God yesterday, today, and forever. You alone are worthy of all honor, praise, and glory. Thanks be to our Lord Jesus Christ.

I know my breakthrough is on the way. I know that you keep your promises. I will see the goodness of the Lord in the land of the living. Thank you that reconciliation, restoration, salvation, and healing for my family are on the way. Thank you for all that you have done for me and all that you will still do. I pray this in the matchless name of Jesus. Amen.

I prayed that twice each day. I did shorten it a little. I cannot put all the names of my family, friends, and prayer warriors, but they know who they are.

I can tell you by experience that you must speak life over your prayers. Speak God's promises over your life. When I started to focus more on the promises of God versus my marital problems, I felt more confident and assured that all would be well. The hardest thing for me was this waiting season when it looked like nothing was changing. But when it's silent, God is moving. We just don't see it. That is why we must walk by faith and not by sight.

My daily verse on February 20 read:

I have told you all this so that you may have peace in me. Here on earth you will have many trials and sorrows. But take heart, because I have overcome the world.—John 16:33 (NLT)

I was uplifted by watching a devo on YouTube titled "God Is Telling You to Be Patient for That Person. Watch for These Signs in Your Heart" by Uplifting Mind.

I have to say after reading all my devo messages and daily scriptures, I was overwhelmed with gratitude. God was speaking to me. I always have peace. I'm so thankful for it. I did get weird anxiety chest pains when something didn't feel right. When I had that anxious feeling, as soon as I changed my decision or thought, it went away. Then the peace came back.

The presence or absence of peace was now my compass. It helps me navigate life now. I feel more confident, knowing that the constant peace is a sign that I am aligned with God's will for my life.

I have been feeling a shift lately. It's hard to describe what I'm going through. These past few weeks have been different. I feel like something is happening in me again. I'm just not sure what it is. It's like every day I'm being chiseled. I am not thinking of my husband as often, though of course, I still miss him like crazy.

February 21, my daily verse read:

Then you will experience God's peace, which exceeds anything we can understand. His peace will guard your heart and mind as you live in Christ Jesus.—Philippians 4:7 (NLT)

A few days later, this YouTube devo was on my phone in the morning when I woke up.

"3 Signs God Wants You to Hold on to Them"

1. Every time you try to move on, something keeps pulling you back to them in a way that feels deeper than emotions. God doesn't let go of what He intends to keep in your life. (Ecclesiastes 4:12)

2. You continue to see growth and transformation in both yourself and them. When God is preparing two people for something greater, He refines individually first. (Philippians 1:6)

3. Your prayers for clarity keep leading back to peace, not confusion. God confirms what He ordains through signs of stability, not doubt. (Isaiah 26:3)
   I texted Matt at 7 pm:

Hey. Have you gone awol on me again? LOL I just need to know if you want to film this week. I am good Tues-Fri. Monday might rain. Let me know what you think. I'm really happy that the bobble heads sold out. I knew they would. Also, I would like to see Yoona. It's all good for her to come over now. Anya is healed. [Anya is my daughter Alyssa's dog.] I hope you're doing good! You are doing an amazing job keeping up with everything. If you need me for anything, I am here to help. ☺

No response.

On February 27, my daily verse read:

But as for me, I will sing about your power. Each morning I will sing with joy about your unfailing love. For you have been my refuge, a place of safety when I am in distress.—*Psalm 59:16 (NLT)*

Matt texted:

Can you film tomorrow in Ocala? Or Saturday?

I texted:

I will be in Ocala with my publisher all weekend. If you want to film tomorrow, please let me know. I will be there at 10 am tomorrow. We need to get to work.

No response.

On February 28, I watched a devo on YouTube by Pure Inspirational:

"5 Signs God Removed Them, But They Will Come Back One Day"

1. Your heart still feels a connection to them despite the time and distance God allows this bond to remain because their role in your life isn't finished. (Isaiah 41:10)

2. You notice signs or reminders of them when you least expect it. These moments are God's way of letting you know that their absence is temporary. (Isaiah 43:18-19)

3. People around you mention their name or bring up memories without knowing how it affects you. God often uses others to confirm what He's preparing. (Proverbs 11:14)

4. Your prayers for their happiness and well-being come from a place of love, not regret. This shift in your heart shows that God is preparing you both for a healthier future together. (James 5:16)

5. Their absence has helped you grow emotionally and spiritually in ways that will benefit the relationship if it's restored. God removes people to help you both mature separately. (James 1:4)

I texted Matt:

I'm taking the no response as a no?

Matt texted:

I will see you at 10 am.

I texted:

I'm sorry I will be late. I didn't think you wanted to work. I will have to charge my car. I'll text you when I'm done charging and on my way.

Matt texted:

Sounds good.

That was the first time I saw Matt since the Tampa RV Show. When I saw him, I couldn't believe how thin he looked. He looked so much healthier and handsome—still stressed though. We recorded three videos, managing to laugh and have a good time. I thanked God that I still got to see him sometimes.

After we were done recording, we decided the following week we would film a lot more. I left for home because I had a busy weekend. While I was driving, I noticed I was in a very good mood. I felt very confident in my God about restoration for our marriage—even though I didn't see anything changing.

I felt happy, at peace, excited for the first time in a long time. I was going to be videoing some interviews with my book publisher, Jennifer, that weekend. We also were going to do a video on three RVs I thought she would like.

March 1 was a really fun day for me. I met with Jennifer at General RV in Ocala. She flew down from Pennsylvania to do some interviews with me about the book process, and I also showed her some RVs that I thought would be good for her to consider buying because her brand and YouTube channel is the Traveling Publisher. We wanted the videos to be helpful and to show the RV from a consumer perspective.

It was a lot of fun to film those videos with Jennifer. I knew she will be purchasing an RV very soon, and I hoped this would help her on her journey. We also filmed four interviews about my experiences writing and publishing my book. Those videos will be very helpful to anyone who wants to write a book.

I had a great day with Jennifer and was grateful she came to Florida. She has always encouraged me and supported me through the journey that I am on.

On March 4, I went to Tampa to film with Matt. Because the Ocala show was in a few days, we were trying to get a good amount of videos done. I noticed Matt was very on edge, preoccupied, and stressed.

It was strange for me to see him like that all the time now. He never used to be like that. It seemed like since we had been apart, he had changed. I didn't know what he was going through because he didn't tell me anything.

It was a bit more challenging to film that day because Matt was kind of short with me and impatient. I didn't think it was me. I felt like it was business. It hurt to see him so stressed and unhappy. After we were done, I got in my car and drove home. We talked about recording after the Ocala RV Show ended, which meant I probably would see him sometime the week of March 10.

On my way home, I didn't cry. I felt like I was being so patient. How much longer can I endure this? I was fighting for this marriage every day. I knew that I could quit and give up. But after all this time, no way! God did not bring me this far to leave me here.

I knew that the enemy was trying to sow doubt and put thoughts in my mind. I prayed to God to help me hold on to His promises because I was so exhausted and weary in this waiting season. Around fifteen minutes after praying, I got a message on my YouTube:

Every time you try to walk away, you feel an unshakable pull that tells you to be patient. God often asks you to wait when there's still work to be done before things come together. (Psalm 27:14)

You keep receiving confirmation through prayer, dreams, or unexpected signs that this person is meant to be in your life. When God speaks, He sends clear messages that are impossible to ignore. (Isaiah 30:18)

They are growing and changing in ways that show God is still working on them. Sometimes, the waiting season is about preparation, making sure both of you are ready when the time is right. (Philippians 1:6)

Thank you, God. You are good all the time. I needed that. God is amazing all the time. His ways are not our ways. He will answer us in many ways. But do we listen?

My March 5 daily devotion read:

God Needs Our Faith

Recently I was talking with the Lord, and I told him something that I needed him to do for me. Immediately, I heard in my spirit, "I need your faith!" This was quite an eye-opening statement for me. Through these words, I realized that somehow, I had weakened in faith and was asking God for help, out of need and desperation rather than in faith. We can ask God for many things yet fail to attach our faith to our requests. I encourage you to ask in faith, believing that God hears you and wants to meet your need. If you know a scripture on which you can base your request, you can remind God that you believe it and that you trust Him to keep His promises. Praying the word or filling your prayers with Scripture is a good thing to do. When we humbly remind God of His Word, it shows we are putting our trust in it and in Him. It also strengthens our faith while we wait for Him to answer us. And whatever you ask for in prayer, you will receive, if you have faith. (Matthew 21:22)

I felt very different at that time—lighter and more carefree. The shift had been happening little by little. I noticed it over the past few weeks. I wasn't sure what it was yet.

The next day, my daily verse read:

Then the LORD God said, "It is not good for the man to be alone. I will make a helper fit for him."–Genesis 2:18 (NLT)

Daily devotion:

The Blessedness of Possessing Nothing

God is the owner and possessor of all things. When we begin to develop an ownership mentality, we do so out of pride, having forgotten that everything we have is a gift from God and that we are merely stewards of His possessions. The words me and mine are all too familiar in our thoughts and conversations. I have come to realize that this ownership mentality is not pleasing God and that we regularly need to lay everything on the altar of sacrifice and make sure that God alone is on the throne of our hearts. When we possess nothing, we can enjoy everything without the fear of losing it or the fear that someone will take it from us. What do you think you own—your ministry, your business, your family, your money, or your material possessions? Remind yourself today that without God, you are nothing and you have nothing. When God gives you something, be thankful. When He requires it back, release it without self-pity. And always remember that as long as you have Jesus, you have everything you will ever need. For the whole earth is the Lord's and everything that is in it. (Corinthians 10:26)

God is speaking to me. I have stronger faith and more joy in the past few months. This is amazing! Something is changing in me.

My devo from YouTube was "3 Major Signs God Removed Someone, but a Reunion is Coming"

1. Even though you are apart, there is a strong sense that your story isn't finished. When God separates people for a season, He often leaves an undeniable feeling of unfinished business. (Ecclesiastes 11:6)

2. You both experience unexpected growth, healing, and transformation after the separation. Sometimes, God removes someone temporarily to prepare both of you for a better future together. (Hosea 6:1)

3. God keeps placing reminders, dreams, or divine encounters that make it clear this person is still part of His plan for your life. When a reunion is in God's will, He will make sure you don't miss the signs. (Isaiah 55:11)

My March 12 daily devo:
Turn Worries into Prayers
Whatever you might be tempted to worry about today, I encourage you to turn that worry into prayer. Worrying produces nothing but anxiety and tension in our souls. That never brings an answer to our problems, but our prayer opens the door for God to work marvelous wonders. One sincere prayer offered in faith can produce more good than a lifetime of worry and anxiety. When you pray, be sure to give thanks along with your requests, expressing gratitude for the amazing things that God has already done in your life. Thanksgiving opens the windows of heaven, but complaining opens a door for the enemy. We can all find things to complain and murmur about, but grumbling is as useless as worrying. Prayer is your opportunity to receive God's help, so take advantage of that opportunity today and every day of your life. Do not fret or have any anxiety about anything, but in every circumstance

and in everything, by prayer and petition with Thanksgiving, continue to make your wants known to God. (Philippians 4:6)

March 14 daily verse:

If you need wisdom, ask our generous God, and he will give it to you. He will not rebuke for asking.-James 1:5 (NLT)

My March 15 daily devo:

How Can I Change?

Our love for Jesus makes us want to be everything He wants us to be. Because of that, we often fall into the trap of trying to change ourselves rather than trusting God to change us. I spent many frustrating years, striving in my flesh (my own strength, ability, energy, and effort without God), to do what only He could do in me. No doubt, all of us need to change and become more and more like Jesus. This will happen little by little as we study His Word and fellowship with Him. God has called you to Himself, and only He can complete by His Spirit what He begins in the Spirit. He is the Author and the Finisher of your faith and of all the work that needs to be done in you. (Hebrews 12:2) Tell Jesus your desire and then lean on Him to bring it to pass. Don't be frustrated with yourself because you are not all that you want to be. God will meet you where you are and help you get to where you need to be. Are you so foolish and so senseless and so silly? Having begun with the Holy Spirit, are you now reaching perfection (by dependence) on the flesh? (Galatians 3:3)

Today was the announcement of Liquified making it into 1,700 Walmart stores nationwide. Matt and Wil did a video and posted it on social media. I was so happy and proud of them both to see them accomplish such a remarkable feat in a short amount of time. They worked extremely hard. We truly have been blessed by God in this endeavor.

The past few days of filming with Matt had gone pretty well. We were getting along very well, although he was still so focused on work. I didn't know what to think about that. I was in a place where I was doing good. I didn't ask Matt questions anymore. I figured

I would leave it to Matt. I trust God will move in him when it is time.

My March 16 daily devo read:

Seasons of Testing

We all experience seasons of testing, times when our difficulties last longer than we feel we can endure, or when we face multiple challenges at the same time. I have been dealing with sciatica for a while now. If you have ever had it, you know that it hurts! I trust that God will take care of it, but while I am waiting it is testing my faith. Paul had a thorn in his flesh, and he wanted God to remove it. But God told him that His strength showed itself most effective through Paul's weakness. (2 Corinthians 12:9) In other words, even though Paul was dealing with a challenge, God promised to give him the strength to do what he needed to do. If you are in the midst of trials of any sort right now, I encourage you to receive God's strength while you wait on your total deliverance. He is standing by ready to help. Consider it wholly joyful, my brethren, whenever you are enveloped in or encounter trials of any sort, or fall into various temptations. (James 1:2)

That was a very ironic devo because that had been my life for the past ten months. I had been in a time of testing and waiting. I am in awe of God every day and the different ways He will speak to me. I often pray for clarity and strength to hold on. Then before I know it, He answers. Sometimes it's not immediately. It could be a few hours or days.

I remember one time I prayed for the restoration of my marriage, and I got this overwhelming peace that invaded my heart. It was a calm reassurance that my prayer was answered.

If you are praying for answers, be patient. God hears and answers our prayers. They might not be the answers we want, but He knows what's best for us.

On March 19, I watched a helpful YouTube devo:

"3 Evident Signs God Is Telling You to Wait on Someone"

1. No matter how much you try to move on, you don't feel peace in letting go. God often places a stillness in your heart when He wants you to remain patient for someone. (Psalm 37:7)

2. Their personal growth and your own keep aligning in ways that make timing the only barrier. When God is at work, He develops both of you separately before bringing you together. (Philippians 1:6)

3. Opportunities to reconnect keep appearing without force or manipulation. When waiting is part of God's plan, He will allow moments that confirm it's not over yet. (Isaiah 40:31)

All these incredible messages I got encouraged me so much. Despite what was happening in our relationship, I never felt that our marriage was over. The little time I saw Matt, I felt our strong connection. I will not give up. I have been faithful and obedient. I know God is faithful, and He keeps His promises. Maybe most people would have walked away by this point. But from the beginning, something told me to fight for this marriage. Even if Matt wasn't.

The past few nights I had dreams about my husband. One was about us trying to figure out a sleeping arrangement for a show or rally. In my dream, Matt said to me, "Let it happen." Then I woke up. I think our dreams are a way for God to speak to us. If we can't discern the meaning or message of a dream, we can ask God for understanding and clarity.

My March 21 daily devo was about:

The Right Time to Be Thankful

Jonah had disobeyed God and was swallowed by a huge fish. But while he was still suffering greatly in the fish's belly, he began to give thanks to God. Soon, he was delivered. It is significant to me that he didn't wait to give thanks until after he had his victory, but he offered a sacrifice of thanksgiving and praise in the midst of his difficulty. Anytime and all the time is the right time to give thanks to God, but it is especially important that we don't forget to do so while we are in the wilderness times of our lives. It is easy to be thankful when our circumstances are joyful and exciting, but it is a sacrifice to do so when there appears to be nothing for which we can thank God. Thank God today for His presence in your life, and know that your deliverance will come at the right time. But as for me, I will sacrifice to You with the voice of thanksgiving. I will pay that which I have vowed. Salvation and deliverance belong to the Lord! (Jonah 2:9)

I noticed something had changed in me over the past few weeks. Each day, there were small shifts and a stirring in my heart and soul. I felt lighter. Sometimes I would be joyful all day, even giddy. I was in love with life. I started to laugh a lot again and talked to everyone.

I would make my Zumba classes crack up laughing. People would tell me that I looked different. I was told I was like the sunshine. Everywhere I went, I was genuinely happy to be there. I spent a lot of time with friends and my daughters. I helped my youngest daughter look at colleges and decide on one. I was finishing up my book.

Then one night I was praying, and I felt what it was: I was complete. God had restored me. He had made me whole.

It had been happening little by little over the past few weeks. I was no longer broken. I was completely restored—whole and healed. Praise God: He keeps His promises.

When God restores you, it's better than anything you could hope for. This was my deliverance.

A New Beginning

Looking back at the most difficult, intense, painful season of my life, I know that my pain had a purpose. So many things needed to change in me. I was barely living my life and neglecting my husband and marriage.

None of us wants to go through that kind of breaking. But it is through the breaking that God transforms you.

Do not conform to the pattern of this world, but be transformed by the renewing of your mind.–Romans 12:2

God's process of breaking, isolation, purification, refining, waiting, testing, and restoration was long and hard, painful and intense. But I was able to see all the things I did wrong and took for granted from God's perspective. I now understand that we must grow with the pain. The stretching reveals what needs to be changed and strengthens our faith.

The process is like a diamond forming. They too go through a process of high heat and pressure, cutting, shaping, refining, then polishing.

That is very similar to what I went through in my transformation. I went through so many stages to get where I am now. If I went against the pain, I would not have grown into who I was called to be. I thought that when my heart was shattered into pieces, it would never be whole again. Many days, I didn't think I could go on any more. But I trusted in God. I leaned into Him. He was my refuge and my strength. Every day he gave me the strength and grace to go on.

Each day I was slowly changing. As time went on, I began to see things about myself that I couldn't believe, such as how I was so much more patient and compassionate. Forgiveness became easy for me. God literally changed my heart. When God spoke to me about my divine purpose to write this book, I wanted to do this—to be obedient to God, and also because in my heart I wanted to help others.

I cannot imagine anyone going through such brokenness without God. My pain had a purpose—to show that all I went through made me the best person I can be. God made me who I am supposed to be in Christ. I am forever grateful to our Lord for what He has done. I give all power and glory to Him forever. I am irrevocably changed. I am joyful, peaceful, and truly content. The calm is with me every day. That in itself is a blessing from God. I literally feel the light of God radiating from within me. My purpose in this life is to be a light to others in the dark and to encourage them. I believe that this was the breakthrough I needed. I am looking forward to what surprises God has in store for me. I will hold on to his promises because I know He is faithful.

We can get through storms and seasons in life if we have the Lord. He gives you peace so you can withstand it. That didn't happen for me right away because I wasn't following the Lord like I should have. I didn't know how to fully surrender to Him. If you pray for His will to be done and surrender, He will give you peace. Always seek his kingdom first.

Now I need and depend on the Lord for everything. I know I can't do this life without Him. I am grateful for each day of my life, excited to see what each day will bring. God has shown me how to love others—not just my family and friends, but everyone.

I don't regret this season and what happened that caused the breaking. God is in control of everything. He sees the end from the beginning. This storm made me better—not bitter. I would not take away my time in the valley for the world. This is who I was called to be.

I know God will continue to restore everything in my life. True love is proven when it is tested. I will continue to fight and stand for my marriage with the confidence that God has already restored us. God can do anything. There is nothing impossible for him. (Luke 1:37)

My dear friend, I pray that if you are going through a tough season or storm that you would lean into and depend on God. Trust Him. Read His Word. He never leaves us nor forsakes us. (Joshua 1:5) Remember the power of words over your lives. They can give life or death. (Proverbs 18:21) Speak God's promises over your life. He wants us to speak them. He is faithful in all of his promises. (Psalm 132:2) When you remind God of his promises, you are showing an act of faith, which pleases God.

Most important is to pray. Prayer is what gave me strength and direction. If you start your morning thanking God for your day, the rest of your day will be good. Pray without ceasing. (1 Thessalonians 5:17) Pray and talk to God when you're driving or in quiet moments. He knows we have lives and are busy, but it will be a lot better for you if you make time for prayer. Remember that God loves you. Nothing can separate us from the love of God. (Romans 8:38-39)

May the love and peace of the Lord be with you always. God Bless!

Acknowledgments

Thank you to my daughters, Kayla, Alyssa and Arabella, and my son-in-law, Joe, for being so loving and understanding through everything. Thank you to Danielle, my aesthetician, who gave me so much comfort and support. Thank you to my publisher, Jennifer Bright, who believed in me and encouraged me to write this book. A special thanks to Ella Stover for the amazing book cover images!

Thank you to my friends who make me laugh and remind me that I am a child of God, full of light and love.

Most importantly, thank you to all of my prayer warriors who have been praying for Matthew and me. I'm deeply touched and overwhelmed by your kindness and compassion.

Last but not least, thank you to my husband, Matthew, my forever love, for supporting me in writing this book.

About the Author

Andrea Foxcroft is a YouTube Influencer and the co-owner of Matt's RV Reviews and a co-owner of Liquified RV Toilet Treatment. Andrea has three daughters, Kayla, Alyssa and Arabella, from a previous marriage and four pets Yoona, Ezra, Yoko and Anya. She is married to Matt Foxcroft. When not creating content for YouTube and writing, she loves to dance, read, travel, rving and interior design. She also likes to visit historical cities and castles. Her passion is motivational speaking. She continues to mentor and encourage others. Andrea currently lives in 'Land O' Lakes, Florida with her two daughters. She is strong in her Christian faith. This is her first published book. She hopes it inspires other readers to share their stories.